PREDATORY THINKING

Dave Trott is the author of *Creative Mischief* and currently
Chairman of The Gate London, part of The Gate Worldwide.
Born in east London, he went to art school in New York
on a Rockefeller Scholarship. From there he began an
illustrious career in advertising, as part of the creative team
behind 'Hello Tosh Gotta Toshiba', 'Aristonandonandon',
'Lipsmackinthirstquenchin . . . Pepsi', the Cadbury Flake ads
and many, many more.

Dave's agency Gold Greenlees Trott was voted Agency of
the Year by *Campaign* magazine, and Most Creative Agency
in the World by *Ad Age* in New York. In 2004 he was given
the D&AD President's Award for lifetime achievement
in advertising.

By the same author

CREATIVE MISCHIEF

DAVE TROTT

PREDATORY THINKING

A MASTERCLASS IN OUT-THINKING

THE COMPETITION

PAN BOOKS

First published 2013 by Macmillan

First published in paperback 2014 by Pan Books
an imprint of Pan Macmillan
The Smithson, 6 Briset Street, London EC1M 5NR
EU representative: Macmillan Publishers Ireland Ltd, 1st Floor,
The Liffey Trust Centre, 117-126 Sheriff Street, Upper
Dublin 1, DO1 YC43
Associated companies throughout the world
www.panmacmillan.com

ISBN 978-1-4472-8534-2

13

A CIP catalogue record for this book is available from the British Library.

Printed and bound by CPI Group (UK) Ltd, Croydon, CR0 4YY

Visit **www.panmacmillan.com** to read more about all our books
and to buy them. You will also find features, author interviews and
news of any author events, and you can sign up for e-newsletters
so that you're always first to hear about our new releases.

CONTENTS

CONTENTS

PREDATORY THINKING

INTRODUCTION:
WHY PREDATORY THINKING?

Over the decades I've worked in advertising, I've learned one big lesson about creativity in particular and life in general.

Nothing exists in limbo.

Everything exists in context.

Nothing is simply good or bad.

It's either better or worse than the alternatives it's compared to.

And yet 90% of thinking ignores the context.

Which is why most thinking doesn't work.

What works is out-thinking the problem.

Faced with a problem you can't solve, get upstream and change the context.

Change it to a problem you can solve.

Henry Ford said, 'There's no problem that can't be solved if you break it down into small enough pieces.'

So get upstream and break it into smaller pieces and see which piece is the pressure point.

Which piece can be changed, that changes everything else.

•

I've never learned much from textbooks.

I find them dull.

The sort of books that break things down into a dry-as-dust formula.

The 8 truths, or the 12 principles, or the 10 essential thoughts.

Rules you forget almost immediately.

For me, that's not interesting, that's not creative, that's not thinking.

One of my advertising heroes, Bill Bernbach, said, 'Principles endure, formulas don't.'

Lessons that you work out for yourself are much more powerful than rules you memorize parrot-fashion.

They stay with you.

That's why this book is a series of stories instead of a list of rules.

Stories that have influenced me, and that I've learned predatory thinking from.

Examples in as many different areas as possible.

That way, you'll learn the principles and apply them for yourself, in ways I might never even have thought of.

And that is the whole point of predatory thinking.

PART ONE

CREATIVE IS AN ADJECTIVE NOT A NOUN

The creativity of mischief

There's a story I love about an ex-student of mine.

He was very talented, very creative and turned into a good copywriter.

He did some nice ads and got a job at a leading agency.

The CEO of this agency was rich and famous.

He noticed that Charlie Saatchi was into modern art.

This piqued his interest.

And he decided to get into modern art too.

So he visited all the galleries and saw lots of modern art.

Eventually he found a large piece he liked.

It was an acrylic painting, made up of lots of small, brightly coloured squares.

He had it hung, in pride of place, in his office.

It was very impressive.

My ex-student was thinking about this one night after work in the pub.

When everyone else had gone home, he went back to the agency's production office.

He took a Pantone book and a pair of scissors.

A Pantone book is made up of little swatches of every colour there is.

He took this book to the CEO's office.

He held it up to the painting against the coloured squares.

Then he cut out some exactly matched squares from the Pantone book.

And he laid them on the carpet at the bottom of the picture.

Then he went home.

The next morning the CEO went into his office.

He stood admiring his new piece of modern art.

He called in his PA and pointed out to her the finer points of its artistic merit.

Then she asked, 'What are those squares on the floor?'

He picked them up and examined them.

They were exactly the size and colour of the ones in his painting.

He said to his PA, 'Get the art dealer who sold me this painting on the phone.'

He said to the dealer, 'Look, I've got a bit of a problem with this painting you sold me.'

The art dealer asked what it was.

Controlling his anger, he said, 'Some of the little squares have started falling off.'

The dealer said that wasn't possible.

The CEO yelled, 'Don't tell me it's not bloody possible, I'm sitting here holding them.'

The dealer said, 'I'm sorry, but that can't happen. That's an acrylic painting. The squares can't fall off, they're painted on.'

The CEO went quiet.

Gradually the penny dropped.

He put the phone down.

This was embarrassing.

He'd been humiliated in front of his art dealer and his PA.

And subsequently, the CEO stopped collecting modern art.

And my ex-student didn't wait to get fired.

He found himself another job.

I thought what he did was very creative.

And what made it so creative was the simplicity.

The understatement.

He didn't do, or say, anything.

He just left some little bits of coloured paper on the floor.

And let imagination do the rest.

I think we can learn a lot about the way the mind works from that.

And the human mind is our medium.

The Ship of Theseus

Plutarch used a conundrum to illustrate how the human mind works.

The Ship of Theseus was built to travel to the furthest points of the known world.

During the voyage it was tossed around by storms, battered by wind and waves.

Sails had to be replaced.

Ropes had to be replaced.

The planks in the hull, even the nails holding them, had to be replaced.

By the time the ship returned, not a single piece of it was made from the original material.

So, could that ship still be considered the real Ship of Theseus?

Some people thought not.

Because not one atom remained from the one that left port.

In which case, when did it stop being the Ship of Theseus?

When the first piece of wood was replaced?

Surely not, that's just a minor repair.

OK, how about the second, third or fourth repair?

When there isn't one original plank left, is it still the Ship of Theseus?

Hmmm, probably not.

OK, when does it change, when does it lose its identity?

Some people said it never lost its identity.

It was still the Ship of Theseus.

It had just restored itself bit by bit.

The basic concept hadn't altered.

In which case, what was the Ship of Theseus?

Was it just an idea?

That couldn't be true either, because you could see it and touch it.

So what was the actual Ship of Theseus?

Two thousand years later the philosopher Thomas Hobbes took it further.

He said, assume the crew of the Ship of Theseus didn't throw any of the old parts away.

As they replaced them, they stowed them in the hold.

Then, when they got home, they unloaded them in a big pile on the dock.

Splintered planks, bent and rusty nails, frayed ropes, torn and faded sails.

Now, which one is the real Ship of Theseus?

The beautiful ship that looks exactly the way it did when it left?

(Although not a single atom of the original ship remains.)

Or the rusted, rotting pile of junk that looks nothing like a ship?

(But every atom of it is made up of the original Ship of Theseus.)

There isn't an easy answer.

But most of us would choose the thing that looks like the Ship of Theseus.

At least it floats; it looks and behaves like a ship.

The alternative, the pile of wood and metal and cloth, doesn't do anything.

Without a mind to envision a ship, to build a ship, to use it as a ship, there isn't a ship.

It needed a mind to think up the concept of a ship.

Then the mind shaped matter to fit the concept.

And then the 'ship' existed.

And that's what creativity is.

Having an idea for something that doesn't exist.

Then shaping matter to make it exist.

Concepts aren't sitting around waiting to be discovered.

We have to create concepts, in our minds.

Then we have to make the concept real, out of matter.

Only then does it 'exist'.

Creativity is creating something out of nothing.

The power of ignorance

A few years back, our phone bill was way higher than usual.

I checked through it and one call alone cost £60.

The children were too tiny to use the phone.

Our little boy was about four and our little girl was about six.

That left me, my wife Cathy and the nanny.

I knew it wasn't me, and they both swore it wasn't them.

So Cathy called BT to check.

The operator checked the number.

She said it was a phone call that had lasted about two hours.

Cathy said, 'That's ridiculous. No one here has made a call that long.'

She asked what the number was.

The operator said, 'It's an 0900 number, madam, the sort they use for chat lines.'

Cathy said, 'Chat lines?'

The woman said, 'Yes, madam, have you had a word with your husband? Sometimes men use these lines and . . . er . . . forget to mention it to their wives.'

Cathy put the phone down and asked me if I'd forgotten to mention it.

This was getting silly now.

The chat lines are the little adverts you see in the back of *Time Out* and the *Sunday Sport*.

'Naughty Girls, Up For Fun (And Anything Else)'.

Fair enough, whatever floats your boat.

But, apart from anything else, how can that take two hours?

There was nothing for it but to call the number.

A recorded voice answered.

It sounded like a chirpy, well-brought-up youngster.

It said, 'Hello, this is Jimbo the Jumbo. Would you like to hear my latest adventure? It all started at the airport one day . . .'

There it was, problem solved.

There used to be a comic supplement with the *Sunday Times*, called 'The Funday Times'.

I used to give it to the kids so I could get five minutes to read the main paper in peace.

My son's favourite character was a little aeroplane called Jimbo the Jumbo.

At the top of the cartoon strip was a phone number to call for a story.

My son had dialled the number and listened to the story.

When he'd heard it, he just put the receiver down and walked away.

It must have lain there, repeating Jimbo's adventures over and over, for two hours.

Until someone eventually noticed and popped it back on the phone.

See, the only time he used the phone was talking to either of his grandmas.

We'd never told him you had to hang it up when you'd finished.

We'd never told him it cost money.

He thought it was free, like the radio.

At four years old, you don't even know the world of paying for things exists, or how it works.

You don't know, and you don't know you don't know.

A child's mind works the same way as a grown-up's mind.

We think what we know is all there is to know.

So we interpret everything according to what we know.

Stanley Pollitt, the founder of the advertising agency BMP, had always wanted a little farm in Kent, complete with sheep.

So when he'd made enough money, he bought some.

It was everything he wanted: picturesque and idyllic.

Except the sheep began to get fatter and fatter.

Stanley realized he didn't know the ways of the country yet.

And it was obvious he was over-feeding the sheep.

So he cut the amount of feed down.

But the sheep still kept getting fatter.

So Stanley cut their feed still further.

And yet still the sheep got fatter.

So he cut their feed again.

And one day the sheep all died.

They starved to death.

It turned out they hadn't been getting fatter after all.

Their wool had been growing.

Which may be pretty obvious to someone from the country.

But Stanley wasn't from the country.

And all he saw was the evidence of his eyes.

And we are forced to interpret any situation using the only tool we have.

Our own experience.

Until we know something, it doesn't exist as a possibility.

Once we know it, we can't believe everyone doesn't know it.

And yet there was a time when each of us didn't know anything.

Not a single thing.

In fact there is still an infinity of stuff we don't know.

Maybe, rather than defending the tiny bit of knowledge we do have, we should be embracing what we don't know.

Lao Tzu said, 'The wise man knows he doesn't know. The fool doesn't know he doesn't know.'

We think it's a sign of strength to have an immediate opinion on everything.

But actually all that does is shut down the enquiry.
It can be much more powerful to say, 'I don't know.'

That opens up the way to something new.

Creativity takes effort

Years ago, the UK was being converted to run on North Sea gas.

They had to dig up all the old pipes, all over the country, and lay new ones.

In some cases the pipes ran under houses.

Then they had to come in and dig underneath.

I read about one frail old lady who didn't want to be converted.

She just wanted her house left alone.

British Gas told her it was compulsory.

The main supply pipe ran under her house.

But she refused.

Her neighbours said she was just a little old dear who'd had a rough time in the past.

She'd lived in that house ever since she'd got married, many years earlier.

Unfortunately her husband was a violent drunk.

He'd come home every night, after the pub, and beat her up.

All the neighbours knew it was going on.

But in those days wives didn't complain to the police about their husbands.

They just accepted it quietly.

Then one night, after years of abuse, her husband left her.

He got drunk at the pub as usual.

Came home, gave her the usual slapping, and walked out.

No one ever saw or heard from him again.

This was a mixed blessing for his wife.

On the one hand it meant the beatings stopped.

On the other hand it was shameful for a woman's husband to leave her.

So everyone was very kind and sympathetic towards her.

But all of this cut no ice with British Gas.

They said they'd have to dig under her house, and that was that.

So, as the old lady stood by weeping softly, they lifted up the carpet.

Then they lifted up the lino.

Then they lifted up the floorboards.

And there was a pit with a human skeleton in it.

The skeleton had a crushed skull.

And the little old lady confessed.

One day she'd decided she couldn't take the beatings any more.

So every night, when he went to the pub, she rolled back the carpet, took up the floorboards, and began digging a pit.

Then she put it all back before he came home.

It took many months of hard work.

Just a few hours every night.

Digging a little bit and disposing of the soil.

But finally she decided the pit was big enough.

So, when he came in blind drunk again, she hit him as hard as she could.

With a cast-iron frying pan.

When he went down she hit him again.

And she kept on hitting him until he was dead,

Before dragging his body to the pit and dropping it in.

Then she put back the floorboards, the lino and the carpet.

And she told everyone her husband had walked out on her.

And everyone was kind and sympathetic to the poor thing.

I think what she did was very creative.

Not all creativity happens in a flash.

Sometimes, as with her, it's more methodical.

She analysed the situation.

The primary problem was her husband's violence.

The secondary problem was that she couldn't leave, and he wouldn't leave.

So the brief was defined as:

How could she stop the violence without either of them leaving?

And the brilliantly simple solution was:

He doesn't have to leave, he just has to appear to leave.

Then she actually made it happen.

And that was the real creativity.

The dogged determination to do whatever it takes.

That's where most of us fall down.

We have a good idea but we stop there.

We wait for someone else to make it happen.

If no one does then we give up.

But she didn't.

That frail, frightened lady did whatever it took.

However hard, however long.

Night after night.

Month after month.
And that's the difference.

Unless we make it happen it never exists.

It just stays as another good idea that never happened.

Visual humour

I've always been very short-sighted.

So I've always worn contact lenses.

Years ago I heard about laser eye surgery.

It sounded great.

You could have your eyes fixed and you wouldn't need contact lenses.

You'd have real eyes like a normal person.

Because it was still in the early stages I didn't know anyone who'd had it done.

But I decided to take a chance.

They told me it was a minor operation.

Just a local anaesthetic, and I could go back to work afterwards.

So I booked an appointment for midday at the Cromwell Hospital.

They sat me in a chair and held my eyelids open with clamps like the ones in *A Clockwork Orange*.

Then the laser beam vaporized the top layer of my cornea.

(Apparently they have to burn off enough to reshape the cornea into a corrective lens.)

Then they bandaged the eye up.

I got a taxi and went back to work.

I sat down at my desk and picked up a script, but it swam in front of my eyes.

I couldn't focus.

Some letters seemed really close and some seemed far away.

I kept blinking, trying to get it in focus, but the type kept getting bigger and smaller.

It was like trying to read through the rippling surface of a pond.

I'd move my head back to try to see the bigger letters, then forwards to see the smaller letters.

I was beginning to feel really queasy.

I looked at the other scripts on my desk.

The top one was swimming so much I didn't even look through the rest.

I was beginning to feel seasick.

I looked at the clock.

The face of the clock was rippling with strange wobbly numbers.

I couldn't even bring the clock into focus.

I felt like throwing up.

Obviously my brain must have been affected by the laser treatment.

I wasn't expecting that.

Maybe the best thing to do was get some sleep, and hope my brain unscrambled itself.

So I got a cab, went straight home and crawled into bed.

The next morning I woke up and felt better.

I looked around the room and everything seemed OK.

I got dressed, I went into work.

I went to my desk and all the paperwork was there.

I looked at it and it looked fine.

Everything was the right size, nothing swam before my eyes.

I breathed a huge sigh of relief.

Then I noticed the waste-paper basket was full of crumpled paper.

I fished some of it out and the letters started to swim again.

They were big and small and wobbly.

So I called our secretary.

I said, 'Nicky, do you know what this is about, all this strange, uneven paper in my waste basket?'

She laughed and said, 'Oh yes, Gordon photocopied everything on your desk to appear wobbly.

He wanted it all bendy for you when you came back from your operation. He even did it with the clock face. I told him I thought it was a bit cruel, but he assured me you'd find it amusing.'

And to be fair, he was right.

Some ideas are too good not to do.

Even if they are unkind.

How can we each get what we want?

When my daughter was young, all she wanted to do was watch TV.

She'd sit in front of it hypnotized.

This didn't work for me.

I wanted her to use her imagination, develop her mind.

In short, I wanted her to be learning.

But I didn't want to force her to learn.

I wanted her to have what she wanted.

But I also wanted what I wanted.

This seemed to me just like an advertising problem.

How can we set it up so that everyone gets what they want?

What's a creative way to approach that?

Mainly she loved cartoons.

So I looked everywhere for interesting cartoons that I thought she'd like.

Eventually I found a series of all Shakespeare's plays.

They'd been made by different Eastern European animation companies.

Some were drawn animation, some were 3D stop-frame.

In each case the play had been reduced from several hours down to half an hour.

They kept the main plot lines, and the most important speeches.

Just what I wanted.

It wasn't enough to bore her, just enough to stay interested.

She would watch anything that was animation on TV.

And without knowing it, she was getting a good grounding in the works of Shakespeare.

Stories of love, honour, confusion and betrayal.

All told in fancy costumes and elegant language.

Just the sort of thing to interest a little girl.

I knew it was working when I found her and her little brother in the kitchen one day.

There was a large puddle of milk on the floor and they looked guilty.

I said, 'Who's spilt this all over the floor?'

She stood up straight, looked me in the eye, and said, 'Thou canst not say I did it. Shake not thy gory locks at me.'

How can you get angry with a very little Lady Macbeth?

She was two years older than her little brother.

And little boys are different to little girls.

So several years later, he needed a different solution.

Because I was at work, he would come home from school and plonk himself in front of the TV.

So no homework would get done.

The most obvious solution was to take the TV away.

But what happens when the grown-ups want to watch it?

We needed a more creative approach to the problem.

How to get what we both wanted?

He wanted TV, I wanted him to do his homework.

So, start with researching the market, and come up with a brief.

Two things we know about boys: they love to play games, and they're very competitive.

So how could I make that work for both of us?

Eventually, I thought, let's change all the TV plugs to French plugs.

They've only got two prongs and won't fit into UK three-prong sockets.

So that's what I did.

I bought several French two-pronged plugs, and several three-pronged converter plugs.

You could only use the TV if you also used the UK converter plug.

So, every evening before I went to bed, I hid the converter plug in a different place.

I'd tell him he couldn't have it until he'd done his homework.

Of course, at first, he'd spend an hour looking for it.

Then eventually, he realized he was just wasting TV time and he'd be better off doing his homework.

So he'd do it, then call me at the office, and I'd tell him where the plug was.

Then, before I went to bed the next night, I'd find a different place to hide the plug.

This worked well, and gradually the homework began getting done with as little disruption as possible.

Like all the best creative solutions, we each got what we wanted.

But there's a sequel to this.

Recently on holiday we were talking about this and my son, now a grown-up, told me that actually he knew where the hiding places were.

But he didn't want me to know he knew.

So he'd come home, watch some TV, then do some homework and call me up to ask where the plug was.

Pretending he didn't know.

I was really pleased with this.

Because instead of just getting his homework done, he had been developing his mind.

He'd worked out how to give me what I wanted while still making sure he got what he wanted.

He was working out how to out-think me.

In short, he was learning how to be creative.

A creative mind is an enquiring mind

I recently went to a talk at the Science Museum.

Stephen Hawking, James Dyson, Robert Winston and Richard Dawkins.

Four people who range from merely brilliant to genius.

What I loved best was that as they talked, these brilliant men changed into little boys.

They were bubbling over with fun and playfulness and eagerness to ask questions about the world.

To discover everything they could about their environment.

Dying to share what they'd found out about how things work.

Full of questions and excitement.

The way a little child is knocked out just to be alive.

James Dyson talked about how Frank Whittle invented the jet engine before the Second World War.

And if the government had only listened we could have had jet planes fighting the Luftwaffe in the Battle of Britain.

Robert Winston talked about his medical hero.

Who, around 1780, had been able to remove a tumour twice the size of the man's head.

Without anaesthetic, and without disfigurement.

Predating plastic surgery by nearly 200 years.

Richard Dawkins talked about the man who discovered natural selection at the same time as Darwin.

But humbly gave Darwin all the credit.

It was riveting to listen to these people because they loved what they did.

Dry, dull, academic subjects like science, chemistry and biology came alive.

And gradually it dawned on me what they all had in common.

They all had enquiring minds.

And I realized I was watching not only four very brilliant people.

But four creative people.

Because that's what makes people creative.

An enquiring mind.

As the thinker Edward de Bono says, 'There are many people calling themselves creative who are mere stylists.'

And what separates creative people from stylists is an enquiring mind.

Not just people who want to reshape or restyle an existing solution.

But people who say, 'Why does it have to be that way?'

People who question the question.

People for whom the '?' at the end of a sentence is the most important part of the sentence.

I loved the energy, the buzz, the vitality, the aliveness.

The sense of discovery.

Not just rehashing what other people have done and trying to do it slightly better.

Questioning the very basis of what's being done.

Seeing it doesn't have to be done that way.

The thrill of upsetting accepted wisdom.

Discovering a new way.

A way no one else had found.

Or a way everyone else said wouldn't work.

That's true creativity.

And those four scientists/inventors/philosophers had it coming off them like sparks.

Asking what every creative person should always be asking: 'Why?'

PART TWO

LIFE IS A ZERO-SUM GAME

Predatory thinking

Robert Stanford-Tuck was a Second World War fighter ace.

In just two years he shot down around 30 enemy planes.

In 1940 it looked pretty obvious that Britain was going to lose the war.

Mussolini decided to bring Italy in on the German side.

So they'd get a share of the spoils.

And so Mussolini mounted a bombing raid on London.

This seemed to be working for the Luftwaffe, and he wanted to show that the Italian Air Force could do it too.

Robert Stanford-Tuck's squadron was scrambled to meet the air raid.

He remembers being surprised that these weren't the big ugly bombers, with black crosses on, he was used to seeing.

They were slow, old-fashioned, three-engine aeroplanes.

And they were protected not by deadly Messerschmitt fighters, but by elegant little biplanes.

Very pretty and manoeuvrable.

But slow and under-gunned.

The Italian planes were ripped to shreds by the battle-hardened RAF.

When he ran out of ammunition, one of the Polish pilots even used his propeller to chew the top wing off an Italian biplane.

It was a massacre.

After landing it was customary for a pilot to inspect any kills he'd made.

So Stanford-Tuck got in his little sports car and went looking for the Italian bomber he'd shot down.

When he got to it, he found it had crash-landed in a field.

Stanford-Tuck was used to inspecting Dorniers and Heinkels after he'd shot them down.

Vicious killing machines, where every square centimetre was taken up by weapons, ammunition, dials, instruments and bombs.

But when he got into the Italian bomber he was shocked.

It wasn't like that at all.

There was lots of space to move around.

The seating was comfortable.

There was only a small bomb bay.

The rest of the room was taken up with food hanging from the inside of the aircraft.

Bottles of Chianti, bread, salami, pastrami, cheeses.

Stanford-Tuck said he began to feel strangely guilty.

That he'd shot them down unfairly.

They were just out for a day trip.

They thought they'd fly around for a bit, drop a few bombs, and come home to a hero's welcome.

It seemed they were not part of the serious business of war.

I feel like that about a lot of clients.

They're not part of the serious business of advertising.

Of taking market share from their competitors.

They just want to make a nice commercial that everyone likes.

Or do some nice online films that might go a little bit viral.

Something that everyone quite likes.

But nothing too controversial.

Not messages that will upset the competition.

Not anything that will make anyone uncomfortable.

They don't really want to make waves.

They don't want to cause a fuss.

They don't really want to fight.

Which suggests they're in the wrong job.

Because marketing, like war, is a zero-sum game.

If you want something you have to take it from someone else.

In order for someone to win, someone has to lose.

Adam Morgan described it as 'like a knife-fight in a phone box'.

There isn't anywhere to hide.

There isn't any place for bystanders.

Everyone has to choose.

Do they want to be the predator or the prey?

Because, if they don't choose, the choice gets made for them.

Like the Italian Air Force.

The hard choices

The philosopher Isaiah Berlin said there are two kinds of liberties.

Positive liberty and negative liberty.

Positive liberty is the freedom to DO things.

Go where you want, with whom you want, when you want, etc.

Negative liberty is the freedom FROM things.

Freedom from fear, from hunger, from exploitation, etc.

Both these freedoms are undoubtedly good things.

But people refuse to face the truth about them.

The more you have of one, the less you have of the other.

On the one hand:

If you give everyone the freedom TO carry a gun.

You take away someone else's freedom FROM fear.

If you give everyone freedom TO make money however they want.

You take away someone else's freedom FROM exploitation.

On the other hand:

If you give everyone freedom FROM homelessness, the state must pay for housing.

Which means higher taxes.

Which means someone else loses the freedom TO spend their money how they want.

No one wants to face these hard choices.

If you want more of one, you have to have less of the other.

Remember science class at school?

The most basic rule: nothing can be created or destroyed.

It can only change state.

We can heat a block of ice, and it turns into water.

We can heat the water, and it turns into steam.

A solid, to a liquid, to a gas.

But the same amount of matter remains in existence.

That's the essence of the zero-sum game.

Nothing new magically appears.

If you want it, it has to come from somewhere else.

How come we don't know that in our business?

If we want more sales, if we want to grow the market, if we want to increase brand share, it has to come from somewhere else.

When was the last time you saw a brief that identified where we'd be taking sales from?

When was the grubby subject of money mentioned?

Who would be putting their hand in their pocket and deciding not to spend the cash on that, but on this instead?

How about never.

We talk about branding and hope it will act like a magnet.

Magically attracting people from somewhere.

Like moths to a flame.

No one wants to identify exactly where they're coming from.
Because, like politicians, no one want to make the hard
choices.

You can have it all. But not all at once

My wife's an art director.

So she'd often go abroad on shoots.

This was good for me.

When the kids were small, it meant I had them to myself.

And we could do all the things we couldn't do when Mum was there.

Like healthy eating.

We didn't have to do that.

One time I said to them, 'OK, Mum's not here so you can eat whatever you want. What do you want?'

My little boy said, 'I want Twiglets and strawberry ice cream.'

I said, 'OK, which do you want first?'

He said, 'I want them together.'

I said, 'Are you sure? It might not taste nice.'

He said, 'You said I could have whatever I wanted.'

I said, 'OK, fair enough.'

And I gave him a bowl of strawberry ice cream with Twiglets sticking out of it.

He picked one up and stuck it into his mouth and shut his eyes.

Then he opened his eyes and looked puzzled.

Something wasn't right.

These were his two favourite things: Marmite-flavoured Twiglets and strawberry ice cream.

If they tasted great on their own, they must taste double-fabulous together.

But somehow it wasn't happening.

In fact they tasted worse together than they did separately.

How could that be?

That didn't make sense.

This was my son learning what lots of marketing people still haven't learned.

More is less.

You can't have more than 100%.

It's like a glass that's full of liquid.

Drop something in, and the same amount of liquid overflows out.

It's just displacement.

When you add salty to sweet you don't get 200% taste.

You get something that is 50% salty, 50% sweet.

But it's always only 100%.

You can't add something without taking away something.

The more you have of one, the less you have of the other.

That's why propositions are supposed to be single-minded.

Because, that way, you get 100% of your media spend concentrated on the main message.

Whereas with a complicated proposition you dilute and fragment your message.

Less important points don't add to the communication.

They detract from the most important point.

That's what the single-minded proposition is all about.

That's why we need people to make the effort to decide what is absolutely essential.

Not just people who think of what else they can include.

Welding a JCB to a Ferrari doesn't make a machine that can dig roads at 200 mph.

It makes something that can't do either job properly.

Strawberry ice cream and Twiglets work better on separate plates.

Separate messages work better in separate ads.

PART THREE

90% OF ADVERTISING DOESN'T WORK

No one's even looking

When he was young, my dad joined the police.

On the first day, all the new recruits went into a big classroom.

A police inspector walked to the front of the class.

He told everyone to take out their exercise books and copy down what he was going to write on the blackboard.

As he was writing, another man entered the class and handed him a message.

The inspector put the message in his pocket and carried on writing.

When he'd finished, he turned to the class.

He said, 'Let's see how observant you are.

A man just came in and handed me a message: how tall was he?'

Silence.

The inspector said, 'Nobody? All right, how old was he?'

Silence.

The inspector said, 'OK, how much did he weigh?'

Silence.

He said, 'What colour was his shirt?'

Silence.

He said, 'Did he have a tie? If so, was it patterned or striped?'

Silence.

He said, 'Did he have stubble, or was he clean-shaven?

What colour were his shoes?

When he gave me the message, was he right- or left-handed?'

No one said a word.

The inspector slammed his chalk on the table.

He said, 'You all say you want to be police officers.

That means you cannot behave like ordinary citizens.

You cannot go around oblivious to what's happening.

You cannot afford to switch off.

You must be aware, AT ALL TIMES, of everything that's going on around you.'

Of course none of those recruits had noticed the man giving the inspector a message: that was the idea.

The inspector knew they'd still be acting and thinking like civilians.

Only capable of concentrating on one thing at a time.

That's why he told them to write in their books.

To make the point that people don't notice what's going on around them.

Of course, that affected my dad's behaviour from that point on.

As a policeman, it became his job to be aware of everything.

Especially things other people didn't even notice.

It became his job to notice everything.

Now, unfortunately, in advertising we don't deal with many policemen.

In my job I deal with ordinary people.

People who don't notice anything.

People who are only interested in one thing at a time.

People who are conditioned to filter out distractions.

People who are doing the opposite of what policemen are trained to do.

And yet we treat consumers as if they were all policemen.

Trained to notice every detail of every ad.

The brand personality, the subtle messaging, the ironic subtext, the typeface, the style of animation, the nuances of the humour, the relevance of the music, the casting, the lighting, the editing.

When, in fact, they aren't even looking.

They don't care, and they don't want to care.

They're not trained policemen.

They are sleepwalking civilians.

See, the real issue isn't, is our advertising saying the right things?

The real issue is, how do we even get noticed?

£18.3 billion is spent yearly in the UK on all forms of advertising.

4% remembered positively, 7% remembered negatively, 89% not noticed or remembered.

The worrying number isn't the 7% (advertising doesn't always have to be liked to work).

The worrying number is the 89%.

Because it means 9 out of 10 ads are as invisible as the man who gave that message to the police inspector in front of the class of new recruits.

And, unless we want to be part of that wasted £16.3 billion, we need to change the question we're asking about our advertising.

Because the question we should really be asking isn't, is it right?

The question is, will anyone even notice it?

What's in it for me?

Recently, a young woman called Dani asked me if I'd run a workshop for something called the Young Creative Council.

I said, 'What's in it for me?'

Dani looked a bit shocked.

Obviously, people didn't usually ask that.

She asked me what I meant.

I said, 'You want to learn something from me about advertising.

But you won't learn passively, just by sitting there and listening.

You'll only learn by doing.

So treat this as an advertising problem.

An advertising problem always involves the question, how do we get someone to do (or think) what we want?

So the simple equation is always "What's in it for them?"

That's what we have to work out.

So look at this as an advertising problem.

You want me to come and do a workshop.

OK, that's what you want.

But why should I do it?

How can you make me want what you want?

In this case I'm the consumer.

You're the client, the planner, the account man, the creative team, the entire agency.

How can you make doing a workshop for the Young Creative Council something I want?

Don't answer right now.

Take your time, think about it and get back to me.'

About two weeks later I got an email from her.

The main thing it said was, 'I remember you saying, "What's in it for me?"

Well, I don't think there's much we can offer you that you don't have already.'

So what she's actually said to me is: 'We can't think of any reason why you should do it. But do it anyway.'

Let's just see how that would translate as an agency's response to a pitch.

Suppose we're trying to win a car account.

After two weeks we go back to the client.

I say, 'We couldn't think of anything, so here's our campaign.'

And we show them a poster with the headline:

'WE CAN'T THINK OF ANY REASON YOU SHOULD BUY THIS CAR, BUT PLEASE BUY IT ANYWAY.'

How likely is that poster to work?

How likely is the client to run it?

How likely are we to win the pitch?

In fact, how likely are we to keep our jobs?

It wouldn't be a very professional thing to do, would it?

Because, as a professional, you can never say, 'I can't think of an idea.'

You have to think of an idea.

Simply because you're a professional.

You accept money for doing that job.

And that's how a professional thinks.

Everything is an advertising problem.

Everything is an opportunity to be creative.

Everything is a chance to get people to do, or think, what you want them to do or think.

If you have to sit in a classroom and wait until the teacher gives you a brief then you're not a professional.

You're a student.

Nothing wrong with that, as long as you're happy to stay a student.

But, whenever you're ready to be a professional, you have to give up being a student.

You have to give up being spoon-fed.

And that, if the Young Creative Council choose to learn it, is the first lesson.

That was the workshop.

Believability beats truth

Group Captain John Cunningham was in charge of a night-fighter squadron.

During the Blitz, his squadron shot down twice as many aircraft as any other night-fighter squadron.

Everyone knew the secret.

Cunningham had exceptional eyesight, because he ate a lot of carrots.

Carrots have a lot of vitamin A.

This helps improve perception of light on the retina, and helps it recover quickly after a flash of bright light in darkness.

In those days ordinary people hadn't heard about vitamins.

So this was big news in all the papers.

Cunningham became a celebrity.

He also wore dark glasses in the daytime.

He only took them off at night, to fly.

This was to maintain the sensitivity of his night vision.

Obviously his eyes would be sharper than other people's, who'd been exposed to bright light all day.

So exceptional eyesight made Cunningham a really effective night-fighter pilot.

Well, not quite.

His squadron did shoot down twice as many bombers as any other squadron.

But it had nothing to do with his eyesight.

That was just propaganda.

The RAF had actually developed a combined radar system.

One half based on the ground would guide night-fighters to bomber formations.

And one half in the plane would guide the pilot to an individual bomber.

It was the first of its kind in the world.

And Cunningham's squadron was the first to be equipped with it.

If the enemy found out, they'd take counter-measures.

So the longer the RAF could keep it quiet, the better.

Cunningham became a national hero.

Enemy spies reported back to Germany that the reason they were losing so many bombers was the deadly 'Cat's Eyes' Cunningham.

And for a long while the Luftwaffe bought that story.

They lost a lot of bombers to radar before they discovered the truth.

Because a simple lie is often more powerful than a complicated truth.

At least when it comes to mass communication.

It didn't matter that it wasn't true.

All that mattered was, did the target market want to believe it?

And, for most people, something that captures the imagination is more powerful than something that captures reason.

Margaret Thatcher was a master of this.

That's why she won three elections in a row.

I once heard her on TV talking about the economy to a BBC interviewer.

He asked her exactly why she overrode her cabinet's advice on financial policy.

She said something like, 'Well, you know, when it comes to money, we women have always had to take charge of running the household.

So I think we are rather better at handling money than men.'

Of course, you could hear *Guardian* readers groaning in disbelief at how crass that statement was.

But you could hear many, many more housewives up and down the country nodding vigorously in agreement.

And there are a lot more housewives with votes than there are *Guardian* readers.

And those housewives understood what Mrs Thatcher was saying.

It didn't matter whether or not it was true.

What mattered was whether the target market wanted to believe it.

That's a big problem we have in the advertising industry.

We're too clever.

And we think clever will always work.

We're all university grads, so we all come up with solutions

we believe will make sense to an intelligent person.

A person like us.

One problem.

Outside Soho, in the real world, most people aren't like us.

They aren't interested in the little bubble of the London

media scene.

And, what's more, they couldn't care less.

So, if we want to do something that works for them, we need

to forget about what works for us.

We need to do something that penetrates their world.

Not something we can believe.

Something they want to believe.

The plumber and the ad man

I was having lunch with Alan Thompson who runs the Haystack Group.

It's a new-business intermediary that places hundreds of millions of pounds of business a year.

But Alan told me something more interesting at lunch.

Alan's dad is over 80 years old.

When the weather got really cold, his dad turned on the central heating.

The boiler fired up, but the radiators stayed ice cold.

The house was freezing.

He had to put on an overcoat, gloves and scarf.

He could see his own breath indoors.

For an elderly person, this is serious.

So his dad went through the *Yellow Pages* and found a plumber.

The plumber came and did the usual thing.

He sucked air through his teeth and tut-tutted.

He said, 'Blimey, this is an old boiler.'

Alan's dad said, 'Yes, I've had it ages.'

Then the plumber walked around and felt all the pipes.

Eventually he took out a hammer.

He hit one of the pipes two or three times and waited.

The pipes began to warm up.

Then the whole house gradually got warm.

The plumber said, 'There you are. It was an air lock in your pipes, that's shifted it.'

Alan's dad was really grateful.

He said, 'Thank you very much. What do I owe you?'

The plumber said, 'Nothing.'

Alan's dad said, 'But I must pay you for fixing the heating.'

The plumber said, 'No, I can't charge you just for hitting a pipe with a hammer.'

Alan's dad said, 'That doesn't seem fair.'

The plumber said, 'Look, this is a really old boiler. With luck it'll get you through this winter, but you'll probably want to replace it soon.

All I ask is that you let me quote on it when you do.'

Afterwards, Alan asked his dad what he was going to do.

His dad said, 'Well, I don't think I'll bother getting any competitive quotes. I mean, even if they are cheaper, I don't know if I can trust them.

I know I can trust this plumber; he didn't rip me off when he had the chance. I'll just get him to do it.'

What a brilliant piece of marketing thinking.

This plumber's not just looking to make a quick few quid.

He's building a brand.

He's worked out what his point-of-difference is among his competitive set.

Which is: he's an honest plumber, you can trust him.

Given that most people are insecure because they don't know the first thing about plumbing.

Given all the TV programmes showing people getting ripped off by plumbers.

Given how vulnerable people are to cold in the depths of winter.

Given all that, this is fantastic positioning.

Of course, trust is the positioning most marketers say they want.

But this guy doesn't just talk it, he walks it.

He invalidated all the competition for a much bigger job, without even a pitch.

And he's got a client who's doing his word-of-mouth advertising for him.

How brilliant is that?

You might say, well, that's OK for plumbers, but what's it got to do with us?

Years ago, Nigel Bogle was running TBWA.

Clients occasionally came to see him when they were in trouble.

When the work their current agency presented was unusable.

And they needed to be on air with a new campaign in a matter of weeks.

Nigel would listen to their problem.

Then he'd say, 'I understand your problem and I wish we could help. But I think you've got more fundamental issues than just hitting an airdate in the short term.

I think it needs a lot more strategic thought.

If we did a quick fix for you I don't think it would benefit either of us.

We wouldn't be doing our best work, and you'd be disappointed.

But, I can understand that you do have commercial imperatives and you need to hit that deadline.

So, if you'd like, I can help you pick an agency that will do a reasonable job in the short term.

Then, when you do have a bit more time, we'd love to talk to you again and show you what we can really do for you.'

You might think, he's crazy, he's just given away business.

But has he?

Isn't he actually doing the same as the plumber?

What are the chances of the other agency doing a brilliant job in those circumstances?

Not great.

The very best they're going to do is perhaps adequate.

And what client can resist the thought that they'll never know how great it could have been if they'd got TBWA, and Nigel, involved earlier?

The client has to keep the lines open.

So that later on, he can ask him to have an in-depth look at his business.

And now the whole balance of the relationship is different.

Now Nigel, and TBWA, is a trusted adviser, not just a supplier.

You trust Nigel like you trust that plumber.

Which is why he eventually opened his own agency.

And why Bartle Bogle Hegarty now has offices on five continents, billing £1.5 billion a year.

Never mind the quality, feel the width

My first job in advertising in London was at BMP in Paddington.

We had a lovely old delivery-van driver called George.

George was a little, tubby, bald cockney with a gravelly voice.

He was always wheeling and dealing, always had slightly dodgy merchandise to sell.

One day George came round the creative department looking for me.

He said, "Ere, Dave, you like books, don't cha?'

I said I did.

He said, 'I've got some big books in the van, d'you wanna buy 'em?'

I said it depended who they were by.

George said, 'I don't know nuffink abaht that. But they're three or four inches thick, abaht a foot wide, and two foot long. They ain't half big. D'you wanna buy 'em?'

At the time it seemed odd to me.

Did George really think size was the first consideration in buying a book?

Did he imagine bookshops were divided into two sections?

'Big Books' and 'Little Books'.

If you like books a lot you go in the 'Big Books' section.

If you don't like books much you go in the 'Little Books' section.

That seems silly to us.

But hang on.

If it's so silly, how come we do our jobs that way then?

When I talk to people from different ad agencies all over London, they're constantly filling in timesheets.

To work out how long they spent on a particular job.

Not how good or bad the work was, you notice.

Just how long they spent.

Agencies work out how much of their staff's time the client can afford.

Then allocate people accordingly.

I hear it all over town.

'We can't afford a senior planner on this, we can only afford a junior.'

'The art director can only have half a day on this, we're already over budget.'

'The copywriter can't rewrite the copy, we've spent all the hours.'

And the bookkeeping takes over.

Is that mad or what?

Einstein said, 'Not everything that counts can be counted, and not everything that can be counted counts.'

But we haven't remembered that.

Quite the opposite.

Counting has taken over from what counts.

And we've forgotten the first rule of advertising.

It doesn't matter what went into it.

What matters is what people get out of it.

Imagine if we judged everything else this way.

Films:

'No, I don't want to see that film, it's only 97 minutes long. This one is 122 minutes long, that's a much better film.'

Restaurants:

'Waiter, can I see a menu with information next to each dish about how long it took the farmer to grow the vegetables, and what the chef's hourly rate is?'

Art:

'I don't want to go to the Louvre, the *Mona Lisa* is only 18 inches square. They've got much bigger paintings hanging on the railings outside Hyde Park, let's go there.'

If we're looking for a way to judge value for money, we're using the wrong criteria.

In any other area of life we judge on quality.

How good something is.

It seems in advertising now we can only judge on quantity.
How much do we get?

We're doing our jobs the way George sold books.

The consumer's telescope

When I was young, I used to stop by my gran's house on the way home from school.

We'd have a chat, and she'd make us a pot of tea.

Spooning the leaves from the tea caddy straight into the pot.

One day she showed me a box of teabags she'd won at a raffle at the old people's centre.

We'd never seen teabags, so we didn't know what they were.

We sat around and tried to work it out.

Why would anyone put small amounts of tea into little tissue packets?

Eventually I said, 'The only thing I can think of, Gran, is maybe it's divided into spoonfuls.

So, you know the way you put one spoonful of tea in the pot for each person? This must be like that.'

So that's what we assumed it was.

And every time we wanted a pot of tea, Gran would cut the top off the little packets and empty them into the teapot.

Remember, we'd never even heard of teabags before.

Tea came loose, in a packet.

The thing is, to you it must seem obvious.

You can't imagine a world without teabags.

How can anyone not know what a teabag is?

But that's humans.

We can't believe the world isn't exactly the same way for everyone else, as it is for us.

But the truth is, you only know what you know.

Until someone tells you about something, it doesn't even exist as a possibility.

After you find out about it, the possibility of anyone not knowing doesn't exist.

And then you can't go back.

That's why, whenever I'm in charge of a pitch, the team always sits down together before we start finding things out.

We always write down everything we know about the product, the brand and the market.

At the point we heard we were pitching.

Before we started researching.

Because that is the only time we're ever actually in the same place as the consumer.

As soon as we start to find things out, we move away from the consumer's state of knowledge.

And towards the client's state of knowledge.

And the more we do that, the less use we are to them.

Clients don't need someone who knows everything they know.

They need someone who knows what they don't know.

Someone who can operate, for them, in the consumer's world.

Someone who understands the consumer's mind.

It's like looking down different ends of the telescope.

Clients, naturally, look down the end that magnifies the brand or product.

Until it takes up their whole world.

But the consumer is looking through the other end.

Where the brand/product may be a tiny part, if it exists at all.

How can you operate in a world like that, unless you understand it?

It's that zero-sum game again.

The more you add to knowledge, the more you lose ignorance.

That's a good thing to do.

But you can never go back.

Of course, we can do research groups to tell us in detail what people think.

But these are people we've paid to sit in a room and think deeply about it.

Our advertising never gets to talk to people in this frame of mind.

So that's an artificial situation.

That can take us away from reality.

The reality we had before we started finding out things.

When we were looking down the consumer end of the telescope.

We can't acquire knowledge and keep ignorance.

We want to be knowledgeable about all the client's problems.

We try to know as much about every detail of their brand/product as they do.
So we can impress them.
But it may not help us do the job.
Because the people they want to sell to probably don't know everything the client knows.
And they may not even want to.

We can't assume everyone knows what we know.

Turn the telescope round

Y&R is in the big building at Mornington Crescent, in north London.

But there's another agency in that building, too.

It's an American agency called Wundermann.

Apparently, one day the owner flew in to visit his agency.

He was a big, brash New Yorker.

He drove straight into the car park below the building.

The gruff cockney parking attendant stopped him.

He said, 'Where you going, guv?'

The American was indignant.

He said, 'I'm parking, of course.'

The parking attendant said, 'You gotta permit?'

The American said, 'No.'

The parking attendant said, 'Then you ain't parking here.'

The American was outraged.

He said, 'Do you know who I am?'

The parking attendant shook his head and said, 'No.'

The American got out of the car, raised himself up to his full height, tapped his chest and said, 'I'm Wundermann.'

The parking attendant said, 'I don't care if you're fucking Superman. You ain't parking here.'

I love that story.

I love what it tells us about ourselves.

Our whole world is advertising, so we think everyone's whole world is advertising.

That's why so many of us are so bad at it.

We don't think it's our job to talk to people outside advertising.

We think it's their job to pay attention to us.

So we're not talking to people, we're talking to ourselves.

As Bob Levenson, one of the best copywriters ever, said, 'Most people ignore advertising because most advertising ignores people.'

That's why only the best advertising actually works.

Because it talks to people who aren't in advertising.

But it takes a brave agency to show a client that.

Years back there was an ad agency called Allen Brady and Marsh.

ABM was a very showbiz agency, not very fashionable.

They were pitching for the British Rail account against some very good agencies.

ABM was the underdog.

If they were to stand a chance they had to find a way to prove they knew something the other, more fashionable agencies didn't.

Apparently, on the day of the pitch, the top management of British Rail tipped up at ABM.

They walked into reception and it was deserted.

The chairman checked his watch: they were on time.

He looked around: no one.

Just a very scruffy reception area.

Crumpled newspapers, litter, cigarette ends on the floor, cushions with holes burned in them.

This looked like the worst agency they'd been in.

Eventually a scruffy woman appeared and sat behind the desk.

She ignored them and started rummaging in a drawer.

The chairman coughed.

She ignored him.

He coughed again.

Nothing.

He said, 'Excuse me, we're here to see . . .'

The woman said, 'Be with you in a minute, love.'

He said, 'But we have an appointment . . .'

She said, 'Can't you see I'm busy?'

The chairman said, 'This is outrageous. We've been waiting 15 minutes.'

The woman said, 'Can't help that, love.'

The chairman said, 'Right, that's it. We're leaving.'

And the top management of British Rail started to walk out.

At that moment a door opened and out stepped the agency creative director, Peter Marsh.

He'd been watching everything.

He shook the chairman's hand warmly.

He said, 'Gentlemen, you've just experienced what the public's impression of British Rail is.

Now, if you'll come this way, we'll show you exactly how we're going to turn that around.'

And they took the British Rail management into their boardroom and went through an all-singing, all-dancing presentation of how bright the future could be, if ABM was their agency.

Which, of course, it became.

All by turning that telescope around and looking at it from the other end.

The people's end.

Instead of the advertising agency's end.

Advertising doesn't sell stuff

I always loved Bill Bernbach's advertising for the VW Beetle.

But I never bought one.

I loved John Webster's Honey Monster advertising.

But I never ate Sugar Puffs.

I also loved John's advertising for the *Guardian*.

But I never bought it.

I loved David Abbott's advertising for *The Economist*.

But I never read it.

I loved Saatchi's advertising for the Conservative Party.

But I never voted for them.

I loved Trevor Beattie's ad for Wonderbra.

But I never wore one.

I loved Terry Lovelock's ads for Heineken.

But I never drank it.

I liked Alex Taylor's ads for the army.

But I never joined it.

I like VCCP's 'Compare the Meerkat' ads.

But I've never visited the site.

I loved BBH's ads for Paddy Power.

But I've never been in their betting shops.

I liked Barbara Noakes's ads for Dr. White's tampons.

But I've never used any.

I liked Paul Arden's ads for Silk Cut.

But I've never smoked them.

I liked Fallon's 'Drumming Gorilla'.

But I've never bought a bar of Cadbury's Dairy Milk.

In fact there are loads of ads I love.

But often, I don't buy the product.

So where does that leave advertising?

Does that mean it doesn't work?

Well, it depends on what you think advertising's job is.

If you think its job is to sell products to people who don't want them, then no, it doesn't work.

If you define a great ad as making people rush out and buy something they could never imagine buying, then no, it doesn't do that either.

So how do you define advertising?

I'll tell you what it is to me.

It gives my client an edge over their competitor.

But that's all it is, an edge.

And an edge can't do the whole job on its own.

If you're in the market for a car, maybe I can make you buy my brand.

But you've got to be in the market for a car in the first place.

If you'd never even consider a car, I can't make you want one.

I can't turn a core non-user into a core user.

Because advertising is just one of many factors involved in the process.

Factors like product quality: is it any good?

Factors like distribution: do they sell it near me?

Factors like cost: is it more expensive?

Factors like personal taste: is it available in a colour I like?

Advertising isn't the be-all and end-all of selling something.

True, in a parity situation, advertising can give you an unfair advantage.

But advertising is just one of the factors that will influence selling.

That's why many products sell despite bad advertising.

Because they're good products.

Or they're widely available.

Or they're cheap.

Or consumers like them.

All advertising can do is influence a consumer.

But only influence.

All other things being equal, it can tip the balance.

But it can't do the whole job on its own.

If you've got a good pitch for your product, advertising can get someone to listen.

It can get their attention and get your case heard.

At best it can create a 'propensity to purchase'.

A willingness to buy, a curiosity to try.

If it's available where I shop.

If the price is right.

If it's in my size.

If it's in a colour I like.

If I like the taste.

If I'm in the mood.

If it's the right time of year.

If I'm the right age, sex, religious persuasion.

If I have the right interest, habits, predilections.

If I tick all those boxes, good advertising will work.

But most advertising doesn't work.

Because most advertising is done by people who don't understand that.

PART FOUR

YOU CAN RUN FROM IT OR YOU CAN LEARN FROM IT

How to get laid

The actor Warren Beatty had affairs with many of the most beautiful women in the world.

He was once asked in an interview, 'What is the secret of your success with women?'

He said, 'I ask every woman I meet if she'll sleep with me.'

The interviewer gasped, 'Does that work?'

Beatty said, 'Well, I get slapped a lot, but I get laid a lot too.'

That's great advice about life in general.

When I was a kid, there was a simple motto: 'If you don't ask, you don't get.'

But most of us are petrified to ask in case the answer isn't what we want.

We're terrified of rejection.

We're so frightened of rejection we never ask.

So we never get.

We're guaranteed failure, but that's better than rejection.

Because at least no one knows what we wanted.

We're stopped by thinking too far ahead.

Farmer Jones was ploughing his field and his plough broke.

He thought, 'Farmer Giles on the next farm over has got a spare plough, I'll ask him if I can borrow it.'

And he started walking.

As he was walking he thought, 'I wonder if he will lend me his plough.'

As he walked further he thought, 'He might not. That would be mean, not to lend someone your spare plough.'

Finally he arrived and thought, 'I bet he's just the sort of bloke not to lend his neighbour his plough.'

And he knocked on the door.

As Farmer Giles opened it he said to him, 'You can stick your fucking plough up your arse.'

And that's how most of us deal with life.

We react to situations that haven't happened yet.

What if we get rejected?

What if that beautiful girl says no?

What if the creative director doesn't like my idea?

What if accounts and planners don't like it?

What if everyone thinks it's too risky?

What if everyone thinks I'm greedy?

What if everyone thinks I'm a suck-up?

We don't want to ask a question until we're guaranteed a positive answer.

In advertising, I notice young creatives won't do anything without permission.

Permission.

They won't take a chance on rejection.

But rejection isn't death.

It isn't the end of the game.

It doesn't mean it's all over.

It's just a speed-bump.

That's what an ad creative's job is about.

Handling the rejection.

Let's say half your ads are good.

Let's say the creative director approves half of those.

Let's say planning approves half of those.

Let's say the client approves half of those.

That would be a better rate than most people experience.

Even at that rate, you'd have to do 16 ads to get a good one to run.

But at least now you know the numbers.

If you want 2 good ads to run, write 32 ads.

If you want 3 to run, write 48.

If you want 4 to run, write 64.

And most of life is just like that.

If you avoid the rejection, you avoid the opportunity.

It would be nice if you could always get permission and avoid the rejection.

But that's not how it works.

If you can't handle rejection you limit your possibilities for success.

Whether you're writing ads, borrowing a plough or getting laid.

As they say in New York, 'You gotta kiss a lotta frogs to get a prince.'

Winning is nice, but losing is learning

Randy Pausch was professor of computer science at an
American university.

He was invited to give a speech called 'Your Last Lecture'.

The university invited interesting people to give this talk.

The theme was always the same.

If this was the last lecture you were ever going to give, what
would you say?

What would be the most important advice you could pass on?

The difference was, this really was Randy Pausch's last lecture.

He only had a few months to live.

And he died soon after.

Death has a way of focusing the mind.

So the advice he gave wasn't trivial.

One of the most important lessons he learned was when he
made it on to the football team.

On the first day of training the coach began yelling at him.

He couldn't do anything right, nothing was good enough.

And yet he saw other players getting away with much worse.

Players who couldn't run or tackle as well as he could.

At the end of the day he sat in the changing room really
depressed.

If the coach hated him, why was he bothering?

Maybe he should just quit.

The assistant coach was cleaning up after training.

He said, 'Gee, the coach must really like you, huh?'

Pausch said, 'How do you figure that? He's done nothing but chew me out all day.'

The assistant coach said, 'I know that, that's exactly what I'm talking about.

He thinks you're worth bothering with.

Look at all the other guys he didn't even talk to.

He can see it's not worth his energy trying to make them better.'

That's when Randy Pausch learned that criticism isn't always negative.

Criticism can be a chance to grow.

We always think praise is a good thing.

But praise won't help you grow.

Praise tells you, 'You're doing it right, don't change.'

Praise is a pleasant feeling for a short while.

Dave Morris was an inspirational advertising teacher.

He describes it like this.

'I remember when I was first teaching, Ron Collins was taking a workshop.

He was famous for being a spiky individual to deal with, and part of the way through he came across a piece of work he hated.

My word did he let the student know.

He dismantled the work in fine detail, and then kept referring back to it as the crit progressed.

I was thinking, "You've made your point, the student knows it's crap, leave him alone."

But I was too chicken to say anything.

Fortunately Ron found a piece of work he really liked.

So much so, that he disappeared at the end of the crit and came back with a bottle of bubbly for the student from the agency fridge.

So the evening ended well.

But as everyone was getting up to go, Ron stopped them all and said, "The student who won the bubbly has done well, but that's all he'll remember from tonight – how good he is. Whereas I think the guy over there will have learned the most from this evening, because he's had a good kicking and it hurts, and he'll make sure this never happens again. So I think he'll have got more out of this crit than anyone else."

And he's right.

Enzo Ferrari put it differently.

He said, 'One sometimes learns more from a lost race than a victory.'

Criticism is often more useful than praise.

And we define ourselves by how open we are to learning and growing.

Lazy people don't want to grow.

They just want to be told what they're doing is right.

They're happy to stay on the rung they're on.

People who are good want to grow.

They want to get off this rung and onto the next rung.

They want to get all the way up the ladder.

So they're not looking for praise, they're looking for criticism.

As Eric Clapton said, 'If you're any good at all, you know you can be better.'

You only actually hurt yourself

My dad was a police sergeant during the Blitz.

One day a bomb went off near a school.

Everything was rubble and Dad had to get over there with a couple of constables and cordon the area off.

When he got there the air raid was still in progress.

He found there was a little girl trapped down a hole.

She had her arm caught under a beam.

The rubble from the bombed building was weighing it down.

There was one large wall left standing that could collapse at any moment.

Because they couldn't get the little girl out they called the doctor.

The doctor said he had to get her out as soon as possible, before the wall collapsed and buried her.

But because they couldn't get her arm out from under the beam, he said the safest thing to do was to amputate.

Leave the trapped arm there in order to save her life.

Dad said he wasn't having that.

He had a daughter of his own the same age as that little girl.

He didn't want to see that little girl go through life with only one arm.

The doctor said there was no alternative.

Dad said, what if he hung down the hole and got hold of the beam?

If he could lift it even a fraction, they might be able to pull the little girl out.

They'd save her arm.

The doctor said, what about the air raid?

Just the vibration from any bomb could bring the whole wall down at any time.

Dad said it was worth the risk to save her arm.

So the doctor said, OK, he'd give it one go.

But if it didn't work, he was cutting the arm off.

So dad got a constable to hold his legs, while he hung head first down the hole.

He got a good grip on the beam.

He shouted, 'Ready, NOW!'

And he lifted as hard as he could.

The beam moved a fraction of an inch and they wrenched the little girl's arm out.

It was cut and scratched, but in one piece.

They didn't have to amputate.

Everyone was pleased, and they all walked away patting each other on the back.

Just after they left a bomb went off in the distance and the wall collapsed.

The doctor was so relieved that he wrote a letter recommending Dad for a medal.

In the event, Dad didn't get a medal.

But the constable at the top of the hole, holding Dad's legs, got the George Cross.

My dad always thought that was unfair.

But, like he said, people were dying, it didn't seem worth making a fuss about it at the time.

But he never forgot it.

Last week I was having a drink with a copywriter I really respect.

Someone who's done a lot of good work.

The conversation turned to something he'd done that he didn't get credit for.

He showed an idea to a creative director and it was turned down.

Then a year later, an almost identical idea ran.

The creative director won an award with it.

The copywriter can't forget or forgive that.

He did all the work and someone else got all the credit.

Just like my dad, he's carried that with him for years.

I know what that's like.

I've felt the same, all of us have.

It feels really unfair; you got screwed and you can't let go.

You cling on to the hope that one day you'll get justice.

But inside you know it won't happen.

It's gone, it's in the past.

You're the only one who cares.

When you tell other people, they can't understand the intensity of your feeling.

They even start to get a little bored.

You get exactly the opposite effect of what you wanted.

And yet you can't let go.

That would be like endorsing the injustice.

Or would it?

The injustice is in the past, it's over.

Concentrating on it takes your attention off the present, certainly off the future.

But it's an addiction.

Although you know it's hurting you, you can't stop.

And it saps your energy.

So that the overall effect on your career is like driving a car with the brakes on.

As Gandhi said, 'Revenge is like drinking poison and waiting for your enemy to die.'

Those who can't, teach

When I was young, I failed the 11-plus.

This was bad news, because your future was pretty much decided by this exam.

If you passed it you went to grammar school.

There, you learned English, maths, French, Latin, physics, history and studied for O level GCE.

If you did well, you studied for A level and went to university.

But if you failed your 11-plus, you didn't do any of that.

You went to secondary modern school.

There, if you were a boy, you studied metalwork and woodwork.

If you were a girl you studied typing and cooking.

You left school at 15 and, if you were a boy, tried to get an apprenticeship as a toolmaker in a factory.

If you were a girl you tried to get a job as a secretary, or get married.

That was your future, decided at 11.

So my parents weren't very pleased when I failed the 11-plus.

And it got worse.

I went to pretty much the worst school in my part of east London.

And it got worse.

I came bottom of the class.

I didn't think things could get any worse.

Until the parents' evening.

All the parents had to go along and queue up at the form teacher's desk.

They could all hear what he was saying about each other's children.

My mate's parents were in front of my mum.

She heard the teacher saying that their boy was clever and he should do well.

Then it was my mum's turn.

She asked the teacher what he thought about me staying on at school to do O level GCEs.

When he finished laughing, in a voice loud enough for everyone to hear, he said, 'Keep him on at school, that's ridiculous, what a waste of money. You'd be better off spending the money on a new car.'

My mum was humiliated in front of the other parents.

Then she went home to tell my dad.

He was on night shift, so she had to wake him up to get ready for work.

I knew what was coming, so I grabbed all my comics and went and hid out over in the park.

It was dark so no one could see me.

But I could see Dad driving round the streets in the car looking for me.

Eventually he went off to work and I went home.

The next few weeks were pretty unpleasant.

I never forgot what that teacher said.

That's why I appreciate what the founder of J D Wetherspoon did.

Wetherspoon owns a large range of pubs and hotels all over the UK.

It was founded in 1979 by Tim Martin.

Wetherspoon now has 764 pubs, 16 hotels and over 20,000 employees.

It has annual revenues of £955 million, an operating income of £97 million and a profit of £25 million.

I'm not an accountant, but those figures sound pretty good to me.

The part I like most of all is why the company is called WETHERSPOON.

When Tim Martin, the founder, was at school he had a teacher called Wetherspoon.

Apparently that teacher told Tim Martin's parents that he'd never amount to anything.

Tim Martin grew up wanting to prove him wrong.

But he knew if he just put his own name, Martin, on his pubs, the teacher might not spot it.

After all, 'Martin' could be anybody.

But he knew nobody can resist looking at their own name.

So, just to rub it in, he named the company after that teacher.

Because Tim Martin wanted Wetherspoon to see his own name on pubs all over the country.

And, every time he passed his own name, to know it was put there by the boy he said would never amount to anything.

PART FIVE

LESS
REALLY IS
MORE

Clustering

When I was a junior copywriter at BMP, one of the first commercials I did was for Pepsi Cola.

'Lipsmackin, thirstquenchin, acetastin ... (etc) ...'

I asked the account man, David Jones, how it was doing.

He said, 'Well, it's certainly caught on. But I'm not sure how much good it's doing us.'

I asked him what he meant.

He said, 'Well, I was at a motorway services at the weekend, and a father came in with two young boys.

The father said, "What do you want to drink?"

The boys said, "Two cans of Pepsi."

The father said to the man at the counter, "Two cans of Coke, please."

And the man gave him two cans of own-label cola.

And no one noticed any difference.'

That's how it is in the real world.

We like to think the public inspect all brands under a jeweller's eyepiece.

The truth is they don't.

Sheena Iyengar is professor of business at Columbia University.

She specializes in studying the way people make choices.

In her TED lecture, she talked about conducting research groups in Russia.

As you'd expect, her team provided refreshments for the respondents.

First the basics: cans of Coke.

But, as some people prefer Pepsi, they had cans of that too.

Then, for people watching their weight, cans of Diet Coke.

And, again, Diet Pepsi for people who preferred that.

Then some cans of Sprite, which has a lemon flavour.

Cans of Dr Pepper, which has a cherry flavour.

And cans of Mountain Dew, which has a fruity flavour.

So they laid out a choice of seven different canned drinks.

The interesting thing was that the Russian respondents saw it as one choice.

Cans of fizzy drink.

For them the 'brands' were artificial, just different labels on the can.

They hadn't been 'educated' in brand preferences.

For Sheena Iyengar this was surprising.

She'd grown up in America, the land of the brand.

So she'd assumed infinite choice was everyone's goal.

The more choice the better.

For the first time she saw that was just an artificial construct.

That the mind doesn't see, or need, infinite choice.

In fact infinite choice can be unsettling, disorientating.

Recently, I heard about an experiment conducted in a supermarket.

They set up two displays of spaghetti sauce.

One display featured six different kinds of sauce.

The other display featured 24 different kinds of sauce.

As you'd expect, 30% more people stopped to look at the display with more kinds of sauce.

But here's the bit you wouldn't expect.

30% more people actually bought at the display with fewer kinds of sauce.

Malcolm Gladwell talks about choice on TED.

He says the mind doesn't need and can't handle infinite choice.

The mind works on 'clustering'.

When the choice is over a certain size, the mind clusters the choices into groups.

Because 24 is too big a number to handle, we need to reduce the choice to something manageable, say six.

So we look for similarities and create, say, three or four clusters.

Then we choose one particular cluster and we choose from within that cluster.

What was difficult for Sheena Iyengar, was the realization that clusters take precedence over brands.

People don't choose a brand first, then see what the product is.

They create clusters first, and then brand preference may make a difference.

The truth is we don't want infinite choice.

With infinite choice it's almost impossible to choose.

It's too much.

So we are always looking for a way to reduce choice.

To find ways to knock options off the list.

To get it down to manageable size.

That's what clusters are about.

When I was a youngster, some of my friends used to go to the wasteland near the Thames and collect eggs from birds' nests.

I said I thought it was cruel.

They said it wasn't cruel if there were more than five eggs in the nest.

I asked why.

They said, 'Birds can't count beyond five.

So if there are seven eggs in the nest and you take one, she won't notice.

She'll continue to hatch all the eggs as if nothing's happened

But if there are only four eggs there and you take one, she will notice.

Then she might abandon the nest and all the eggs will die.'

Living beings naturally think in clusters.

That's how the mind works.

That's what makes thinking manageable.

The trick isn't just to increase choice.

The trick is to manage choice.

Everything's changed and nothing's changed

My wife is Chinese, she's from Singapore.

We were about 30 when we met, and I was divorced.

When we decided to get married, we went back to Singapore
to meet her parents.

Cathy's dad had two wives.

Cathy's mum was the younger of the two.

He had three children by his first wife, and five by his second.

When they were young they all lived together in one house.

Cathy told me that, when she'd meet new friends at school, a
common question was:

'Which wife is your mother: first, second, or third?'

She didn't know that this was unusual until she came to
England, to go to art school.

I was brought up in London, so for me this was quite strange.

The concept of one man having several wives.

But of course, when I met Cathy's dad it wasn't something we
discussed.

Because he didn't speak English.

After a few days, Cathy asked me how I got on with her dad.

I said I wasn't sure I was comfortable with the idea of him
having more than one wife.

Cathy said, 'That's funny, because he's not sure he's

comfortable with the idea of his daughter marrying a man who just divorces his wives when he's fed up with them.'

It's strange, seeing yourself through someone else's eyes.

In the West, we've got a system that makes perfect sense to us.

If the relationship isn't working, you call it a day and you both get on with your separate lives.

But he didn't see it like that.

To him, if a man takes on the responsibility for a woman and children, he takes it on for life.

He thought I took marriage trivially.

Changing wives the same way you'd change cars.

When you get bored, trade the old one in for a new one.

But, strangely enough, Cathy's dad and I were fundamentally in agreement.

We both wanted to treat our wives with respect.

But we had very different ways of doing it.

My way was to treat her as an equal, with all the same opportunities, but also the same problems and responsibilities that I had.

His way was to shoulder all those problems and responsibilities himself.

It was a real lesson for me.

We learn to think there's only ever one right way of seeing things.

Our way.

In order for me to be right, I must prove you wrong.

But there's no learning in that.

Just closed minds.

As the philosopher Bertrand Russell said, 'The problem with the world is that the ignorant are arrogant and cocksure, while the intelligent are full of doubt.'

Because thinking is more difficult once we realise there is no right or wrong.

Just the same thing viewed from different perspectives.

STFU

My mother-in-law belongs to a Taoist temple in Singapore.
Sometimes Nepalese Buddhist monks visit her temple to lead ceremonies.
You very rarely see a Buddhist nun.
Except one.
Like the monks, this nun had her head shaved.
She was wearing the same robes.
But what was unusual was that she was a tall Western woman.
In fact this particular nun was an American.
When she had applied to be a nun, there was a problem.
Like all New Yorkers, she couldn't stop talking.
Constantly telling everyone what they should be doing.
What they were doing wrong.
What she liked, and didn't like.
What her thoughts were on absolutely everything.
Eventually the most senior lama gave her an ultimatum.
To become a nun she would have to be absolutely silent for three years.
Absolutely silent.
Not a single word.
If she spoke, even once, she would have to go back to square one and start all over again.

Think about that: totally silent for three years.

That's barely possible for anyone.

Which is why he made it her task.

What the lama was effectively saying to her was: 'Your constant talking is a problem for us. It is very distracting. But we don't think it should be our problem. We think it is your problem. So you need to handle it.'

She had to control the thoughts inside her head.

Get a grip on her own feelings and emotions.

Rather than just dumping them on everyone else.

Have you ever had to sit in a meeting with someone who couldn't stop talking?

Every time someone else said something they had to interrupt, or add to what was said.

Even though whatever they said didn't make anything any clearer.

Usually the opposite.

Just a lot of extra words for no reason.

Why can't people stop themselves talking?

Is it nerves?

Are they frightened of being left out?

I once heard someone on *Desert Island Discs* talking about their life.

They said the most valuable lessons they learnt at school weren't the academic ones.

Every week they would have one hour scheduled, sitting quietly at their desk.

Learning to be alone with their thoughts.

Learning to be comfortable with themselves.

Learning it was OK to be silent.

How great is that?

Most people are frightened to be quiet.

We think there's more power in constantly talking.

Maybe that's why we try to dominate a meeting with more and more words.

Maybe we want to look like we're important.

But if we wrote the way we talk, the page would be covered with so many words it would be illegible.

So why don't we try it the other way round?

Why don't we talk the way we write?

In writing we work out what's essential and just say that.

Why don't we do that with talking?

Work out the most important, powerful thing to say.

Then say it.

Then shut up.

In writing, we know words are more powerful with lots of white space around them.

Words need room to breathe.

So we're more sparing with them.

We only use what we need.

That's what the lama was teaching the American nun.

Only use the words you absolutely need.

In fact, use no words at all for three years, and you'll realize you can get along without them.

Afterwards, you'll only say what you absolutely need to.

Then what you say will be more powerful.

And your speaking will be more than just noise pollution.

You're only ever talking to one person

A year or so ago, I was standing in the agency reception in
Soho reading the *Sun*.

The TV is on, showing rolling news from CNN.

Suddenly there's a newsflash.

A plane had just crashed into a building in Manhattan.

It's only a small single-engine plane.

But, because this is a couple of years after 9/11, it's big news.

No one knows if it's another terrorist attack or just an
accident.

It's hit a building on 72nd Street and 2nd Avenue.

The building's on fire and debris is showering down.

Fire trucks are blocking the street and cops are keeping
everyone away.

I'm watching the pictures broadcast from a news helicopter.

I'm worried because my sister lives two blocks away from
there, on 74th Street and 2nd Avenue.

I check the time difference and figure she would normally be
at work by now.

So I call her at her office on 34th Street.

I'm relieved when she picks up.

I say, 'Hi, Shirl, I just want to check you guys are OK.'

She says, 'Sure, why?'

I say, 'Because of that plane that just hit the Upper East Side?'

She says, 'What plane?'

I say, 'It's on CNN, an apartment block at 72nd and 2nd.'

She says, 'WHAT?'

She calls her husband Jerry, back at their apartment.

He says, 'I didn't hear anything, let me look out the window.'

He looks, comes back and says, 'Gee, there sure are a lot of cops and fire trucks around.'

He goes out onto the street to see what's up.

But the cops won't let him out of his building.

They say, 'Sorry, buddy, we gotta keep the streets clear. A plane just hit a building on the next block.'

And he hadn't noticed.

Now here's a thing.

I'm over 3,000 miles away.

In another country.

On another continent.

And I know a plane has hit a building next to him before he does.

How does that work?

I think we each live in a little world encompassed by our immediate consciousness.

Our context, our surroundings, our environment.

Two blocks away was outside his consciousness.

The room he was in was his consciousness.

And all he's conscious of in there is the music from the CD player.

So the plane crash didn't exist.

Meanwhile, I was in another time zone.

But I had the TV on in the room I was in.

So the news on the TV was in my immediate consciousness.

It wasn't 3,000 miles away.

It wasn't even two blocks away like it was for my brother-in-law.

It was right next to me.

So to be heard, you have to be in someone's immediate consciousness.

That means in an intimate space.

That means one-to-one.

That means, if you're using mass media, you're only ever talking to one person.

You're never addressing a crowd of thousands of people.

Even if the reach of your communication is in the millions.

You're only ever talking to one person at a time.

This isn't new.

This is how advertising's always worked.

Go back to Kitchener's original First World War poster.

The army, fighting the Germans, needed a lot of soldiers quickly.

So they ran a recruitment poster.

But the visual didn't show massed ranks of soldiers.

With the headline, 'THE BRITISH ARMY IS SHORT OF TWO MILLION NEW RECRUITS'.

The visual was Kitchener pointing out of the poster, straight at the person looking at the poster.

And the headline said, 'YOUR COUNTRY NEEDS YOU'.

One-to-one.

And that poster worked.

It got millions of recruits.

By talking to people one at a time.

It was so successful the USA copied it a few years later with a picture of Uncle Sam and the same headline.

And it recruited millions of men there, too.

One at a time.

And that was nearly 100 years ago.

Since then media has changed and changed again.

We've had moving pictures, then talking pictures, then radio, then television, then colour television, then CD players, then MP3 players, then digital, then social media, then whatever's next.

And media's changed and it'll keep changing.

In fact the only thing that hasn't changed is people.

They're still the same.

All anyone's aware of is their immediate consciousness.

That's where media has to reach them.

Whatever the media is.

So we're still only ever talking to one person.

Great writing

For me, the best writing takes complicated things and make
them simple.

So everyone can understand them.

If it's really great, it also takes simple things and makes them
powerful.

So everyone can feel them.

Recently, I was watching a programme about neutrinos.

Neutrinos are a complicated concept.

For a start, they are everywhere all the time.

Millions of them are passing through our bodies every
second.

Billions upon billions passing through our world every day.

The entire universe is filled with neutrinos.

Constantly passing through everything we consider solid.

Just as if it wasn't there.

In fact neutrinos can only be trapped by a certain liquid.

So the Japanese built a massive lake of this liquid, to trap
some.

They built it inside a mountain.

Away from noise, vibration, smoke, sunlight, everything.

Because the neutrinos had no mass they moved through solid
matter as if it weren't there.

Through the top of the mountain.

The sides of the mountain.

Even from underneath the mountain.

But a totally unexpected thing happened.

They found that neutrinos arriving from the bottom of the lake were travelling slightly slower than the neutrinos arriving from the top.

Something was slowing them down.

It was because the neutrinos at the top only had to travel through the mountain.

Whereas the neutrinos at the bottom had to travel through the entire planet.

So travelling through the greater mass was slowing them down.

For the scientists this was shattering.

It changed everything they thought they knew.

This meant neutrinos actually did have mass.

No matter how tiny that mass was.

The interviewer asked the scientist why that was important.

Could he put it into language ordinary people could understand?

The scientist said, 'The entire universe, absolutely all of it, consists of neutrinos.

Many, many more times than that which we consider solid matter.

They pass through us, and our world, as if it weren't here.

And, because they're everywhere, their mass is a far, far greater physical presence than ours.'

This was still a complicated scientific concept.

So once again the interviewer asked, what does that mean to us?

Why should we care?

What the scientist said next fulfils the criteria for great writing.

He simplified all the complicated scientific jargon.

He reduced it down to something incredibly powerful.

He put it in terms that anyone could understand.

He said it in a way that would make anyone stop and think.

Even people who couldn't care less about science.

The scientist looked down.

Then he looked up at the interviewer.

He said, 'It means we are the ghosts in someone else's universe.'

For me, that last line is great writing.

PART SIX

TASTE IS THE ENEMY OF CREATIVITY

Creative charlatans

A man once approached Picasso in a restaurant.

He said, 'I'm terribly sorry to disturb you but I've bought one of your paintings.

It's unsigned and I wondered if I could ask you to verify whether it's genuine.'

Picasso said, 'How much did you pay for the painting?'

The man said, 'Half a million pounds.'

Picasso said, 'It's genuine.'

I love that answer.

Picasso is part genius, part charlatan.

Or, at least, that's how it looks.

In truth, what looks like the act of a charlatan is simply an artist relegating what other people take seriously to a triviality.

Refusing to be restricted by conventional thinking.

Finding it funny, in fact.

Enjoying the fact that every time you outrage conventional thinking, it's another sign that you're on the right track.

Because sometimes, the people you're outraging are exactly the people you don't want to be like.

To them, the rejection of conventional thinking looks like the behaviour of a charlatan.

Picasso said, 'Taste is the enemy of creativity.'

By this he means taste is something we can all see and agree on.

It obeys the standards we recognize.

So we're comfortable with it.

Consequently it can't be new, it can't be creative.

Recognizing this allowed Picasso to ignore the vilification he received.

He didn't worry when people looked at his paintings and said, 'My five-year-old child can paint better than that.'

The fact that philistines rejected him was an endorsement.

Two minuses make a plus.

So Picasso didn't care.

In fact he cultivated the link between creativity and his perceived charlatanism.

That's why he said, 'Bad artists copy, great artists steal.'

Meaning someone who feels bad about being influenced will never make anything that's truly great.

They'll be too busy worrying about it.

Denying it and trying to hide it.

But artists who go through life taking whatever they want from wherever they want will build up momentum.

There's never time to worry about what they just did as they're on to something else.

And Picasso stole from everywhere.

In the early days, Manet, Lautrec, Gauguin, Van Gogh.

Later on Cézanne, Matisse, Giacometti, African art.

This is illustrated by a joke David Bailey once told me.

Q) 'What did Picasso say when he heard Braque had died?'
A) 'Phew.'

Andy Warhol was similar to Picasso.

This was a man who raised charlatanism to an art form.

To accuse him of being a charlatan would have been like accusing him of using a paintbrush.

Outrage was his medium.

Warhol said, 'Art is whatever you can get away with.'

To be proud of being a charlatan is a powerful position.

You have no fear of being found out.

Warhol famously said he loved things that were dull.

He said he adored the trivial and flashy.

He said he loved money.

He said he loved fame.

When critics tried to expose Warhol, they did his job for him.

They'd say his paintings were flashy and trivial.

Warhol agreed: 'Thank you so much. I adore the flashy and the trivial.'

They accused his art of being superficial rubbish.

Warhol was flattered: 'I am deeply superficial.'

Warhol understood that if you occupy the ground first, any criticism merely makes your point better.

Like the original Volkswagen ads by DDB.

The first simply said, 'Lemon'.

Early copy mentioned the fact that people called it 'a pregnant roller-skate'.

They even changed the name of the car to the 'Beetle'.

While everyone else was calling their cars 'Mustang' and 'Cougar'.

The truly creative understand the value of embracing charlatanism.

It means going beyond the fear of other people's opinions.

So if you want to outrage people you can't expect their approval.

They won't like it.

But, then again, isn't that the whole point?

It's OK to feel uncomfortable

At art school in New York, you don't just study fine art.

You have to take some liberal arts classes as well.

One of my classes was in psychology.

One of the subjects we discussed there was Primal Therapy.

It explains that the Book of Exodus is a metaphor for the birth process.

I found that really interesting.

The Garden of Eden is the pre-birth state.

You're in the womb.

Absolutely everything is done for you: food, drink, warmth, shelter.

You don't have to worry about a thing.

It's so safe and nurturing, you don't even need clothes.

All there is for you to do is relax and enjoy.

Then suddenly you're forced out of that paradise.

Into the cruel, harsh world.

Piercing light, screeching noise, people grabbing you, cold air on your skin.

Slapped on the arse.

Choking on the burning rush of air into your lungs.

Change, unsettling, worrying, frightening.

All that security is gone and now you don't know what's happening.

No wonder you start to cry.

Being thrown out of the Garden of Eden is a metaphor for that.

But that's where the metaphor ends.

Because gradually you adapt.

And that new state becomes a great place.

Just watch a toddler.

They want to discover everything.

To pick things up, play with them, put them in their mouth, cuddle them, sit on them.

They've learned the world is a fantastic place.

Now they're not frightened.

Until their first day at school.

Then they cry their eyes out at this strange, unfriendly place.

It's new, it's unfamiliar, it's unsettling, and they don't want to be there.

And they won't let go of Mum.

Fast-forward a few weeks.

They love school.

They can't wait to get there in the mornings.

They start running towards it as soon as they see the playground.

They're off with their friends and they've forgotten all about Mum.

That seems to be the pattern for life.

Try something new.

It's unpredictable so it's uncomfortable.

Then it becomes predictable, so it's comfortable.

Try something new.

It's unpredictable so it's uncomfortable.

Then it becomes predictable, so it's comfortable.

Try something new.

It's unpredictable so it's uncomfortable.

Then it becomes predictable, so it's comfortable.

Somehow, we never quite spot the pattern.

It never clicks that feeling uncomfortable means it's a new experience.

And new experience means growth.

Going somewhere we haven't been before.

Trying something we haven't tried.

That uncomfortable feeling is being alive.

Too often, we want to avoid being uncomfortable.

That's what drugs and booze are about.

Anaesthetize ourselves to the discomfort.

Avoiding confronting it, participating in it, growing from it.

Avoid being alive.

Paul Arden was one of the best creative directors around, as well as a bestselling author.

Paul always used to say, 'It's OK to feel uncomfortable.'

Just that.

It's just a feeling, it's not real.

You don't have to do anything about it.

It just means you're somewhere new.

So you're not comfortable.

But it doesn't mean you should let that feeling stop you.

There's a line I love in *The Jungle Book*.

'You can either run from it, or learn from it.'

In fact anyone who has done anything really worthwhile knows that feeling.

Helmut Krone was maybe the greatest art director ever.

Along with Bill Bernbach, he invented good advertising.

Helmut Krone said, 'If you can look at something and say, "I like it", then it isn't new.'

Don't trust experts

My Uncle Ginger was a marine.

His ship was the *Prince of Wales*, one of the most modern, powerful battleships afloat.

When Japan and Britain were at war, he was sent to the Far East.

The *Prince of Wales* was sent along with the *Repulse*, another huge battleship.

This was called Force Z.

They were sent to protect Singapore from Japanese invasion.

Apparently Churchill was advised to wait while air cover was arranged.

Churchill said something like, don't be ridiculous.

Who ever heard of an aeroplane sinking a battleship?

All the experts said it couldn't be done.

Well, unfortunately the Japanese didn't listen to Churchill's experts.

And they used aeroplanes to sink both battleships.

Uncle Ginger and the surviving crew managed to get ashore in Singapore.

The impregnable British fortress that had the largest land-mounted guns in South East Asia.

All pointing out to sea.

Because all the experts knew Singapore could only be

attacked from the sea, as the land was just impenetrable jungle.

No one could attack that way.

Unfortunately, once again, the Japanese weren't listening.

Their army came down through the jungle and captured Singapore.

The massive guns couldn't be turned around to fire on the Japanese.

Because the experts said they would never need to.

And so Uncle Ginger spent four years in a Japanese POW camp.

The French experts were no better.

They built a massive, defensive fort, practically the length of France.

The Maginot Line.

The part they didn't bother with was the forest at the Ardennes.

All the experts knew it was impenetrable.

So they didn't extend the Maginot Line that far.

But the Germans weren't listening to the French experts.

Their army came through the Ardennes and captured France.

So, not quite as impenetrable as they'd hoped.

History is a procession of 'experts' getting it wrong.

When I worked at the agency BMP, in the pub opposite the office there was a condom machine in the Gents' toilet.

On it was stamped, 'Tested to British Standard 1148'.

Under it someone had written 'So was the *Titanic*'.

People only listen to experts because it saves them having to take responsibility when things go wrong.

They've got a ready-made excuse.

But hang on.

Don't we get good and bad people in every field?

Good and bad car mechanics?

Good and bad plumbers?

Good and bad comedians?

Good and bad artists?

Good and bad lawyers?

So having the right papers, the right language, the credibility, is no guarantee of being good at something.

It's no guarantee of being an expert.

In which case, how do we know who to listen to?

Ultimately, we can't evade responsibility.

We choose who to listen to.

If we listen to the wrong research, choose the wrong strategy, pick the wrong team, we're responsible for the outcome.

Whatever any so-called experts tell us.

We chose the experts.

And we chose to listen.

And, when it all goes wrong, you're on your own.

My Uncle Ginger taught me that.

What works vs what doesn't

As I said in an earlier story, my wife is Chinese – and her religion is Taoism.

In Taoism, clairvoyance is accepted as quite a normal thing.

But I'm from east London.

So I was brought up to believe it's mumbo jumbo.

In fact, anything that didn't obey conventional, ordinary working-class English standards was just superstition.

When we started going out together, Cathy asked me if I'd like to see a clairvoyant she uses.

All of my ingrained prejudices kicked in straight away.

My instinctive reaction was, 'No way!'

But I find continued ignorance lies in reacting.

And knowledge lies in experimenting.

I suspected clairvoyance was just nonsense for gullible people.

Like horoscopes.

But, even if it was, I'd know more about it if I actually gave it a try.

At least then I could reject it from a position of knowledge.

So I went along with Cathy one evening.

It wasn't what I was expecting.

It wasn't beanbags, and incense, and whale music.

It was a sweet little old lady called Nancy, who lived in Uxbridge.

We sat down, had a cup of tea and started to talk.

She said to me, 'I'm getting someone from the other side. A policeman with a little baby on his knee. Do the names John, and James, and Amelia mean anything to you?'

I didn't quite know what to say.

My dad had been a policeman all his life.

Maybe Cathy knew that and she could have mentioned it to Nancy.

But my dad had always been called Jack by everyone who knew him.

No one, except his family, knew his real first names were John James.

And there was something else.

When my sister became pregnant her appendix burst.

The baby was born prematurely and lived just ten days.

It was a little girl called Amelia.

No one outside my immediate family knew that.

I didn't know what to say.

I had been expecting a charlatan.

Someone who would say, 'You are going on a long trip some time in the future.'

Meaningless platitudes that could be twisted to fit any situation.

But this was different, this was pinpoint accuracy.

I find the best position to take in these circumstances is to be agnostic.

Don't be an evangelist or an atheist.

Just suspend judgement, and see where things lead.

On a later visit, Nancy said to me, 'I see you're going to get the Holsten Pils account next month.'

Afterwards, I said to Cathy, 'She's getting confused. We'll get Truman Bitter and David Abbott will get Holsten Pils.'

Next month, while we were on holiday, I got a message from the agency.

'They just gave us the Holsten Pils account, without a pitch.'

I thought clairvoyance was supposed to be just vague predictions that could apply to anyone.

I wasn't expecting names and dates.

A year or so later, Nancy told us we'd have two children, a girl when Cathy was 37 and a boy when she was 39.

I was upset; I didn't want to wait that long, so I ignored it.

We tried for years but nothing happened.

Then when Cathy was 37 she got pregnant.

But she had a miscarriage.

I was furious.

I said, 'So much for clairvoyants.'

But Cathy got pregnant again.

And our daughter was born two weeks before Cathy was 38,
and our son was born two weeks before Cathy was 40.

So where does that leave us as far as a view on clairvoyance
goes?

Well, the mind decides on a position, then makes the facts fit.

So if you want to find a way to believe, you will.

And if you want to find a way to rubbish it, you will.

Like everything else, I think it makes sense to keep an open
mind.

It's the difference between scepticism and cynicism.

Scepticism says, 'I don't believe it until you prove it.'

Cynicism says, 'I don't believe it *even if you prove it*.'

All knowledge lies in scepticism.

Bigotry and ignorance lie in cynicism.

Stop trying to be liked

Jack Dee spent ages trying to make it as a comedian.

For years he plugged away, every night on the stand-up circuits.

Trying to get the audience to like him.

Some nights he'd get some laughs, some nights he wouldn't.

He kept trying to work out what he ought to do.

He tried being cheerful.

He tried being thoughtful.

He tried being nerdy.

He tried being cheeky.

Somehow nothing worked.

And all the while he had to keep his day job as a waiter.

He was getting paid next to nothing as a stand-up comedian.

Meanwhile there were loads of other stand-ups trying to get the audience to like them, too.

All trying to work out what the audience wanted.

All trying to change so they'd be liked.

All waiting for inspiration to tell them what they ought to be doing.

And every night, just like them, Jack Dee would try something different.

And every night some of it worked and some didn't.

And every night he got more desperate.

And he carried on, week in, week out.

He got fired from his day job for being too tired.

He became a drunk from worrying about it.

His girlfriend left him because he became obsessed and boring.

Eventually, it was obvious even to him.

He was crap at it.

He had to think the unthinkable.

He had to think about giving up.

He should accept that he was never going to make it.

And once he accepted that, it was like weight coming off his shoulders.

Now he didn't have to get laughs any more.

Now he didn't care if the audience liked him or not.

He only had one week of bookings left; he might just as well have fun.

So that night he walked on stage as himself, and didn't smile or say anything.

He just glowered out at the audience.

Eventually he said, 'Well, you look a right fucking miserable lot.'

They started to laugh.

He said, 'Shut up, I don't want your pity laughter.'

They laughed louder.

He said, 'Who asked you, anyway? I don't give a fuck. I've only got another week then I'm getting a proper job.'

The audience were laughing, shaking their heads and banging tables.

They'd never seen a comedian like this.

He carried on like that all through his performance.

At the end he said, 'Right, I'm finished. You can all fuck off now.'

And he got a standing ovation.

He did the same thing every night, and the manager offered him a contract at double the wages.

Because Jack Dee did what was actually true for him.

He was himself.

And that was what made him different.

What made him one of the most successful comedians in the UK.

I get lots of letters, emails and phone calls from students and graduates.

Always asking me what they should do to get into advertising.

What does advertising want them to be?

Should they go to college or do work experience?

Should they have a portfolio that focuses on digital, or TV ads?

Should they do mass-mailings or concentrate on top agencies?

What do agencies want?

What do I think they should do?

Can they meet up with me and get my advice?

I think this is a formula for failure.

They are behaving like Jack Dee before he got successful.

They are looking for someone to tell them what to do to be liked.

They'll just end up making themselves the same as everyone else.

It didn't work for Jack Dee, it doesn't work in advertising and it won't work for them.

What works is being different.

Don't try to be liked.

Find out how you're different.

Then be that.

That's where the power is.

That's what's new.

That's what's wanted.

PART SEVEN

THE ART OF WAR

PART SEVEN

THE ART
OF WAR

Fragging

When I was at art school in New York, I knew a guy who was there on the GI Bill of Rights.

This meant he served his time in the armed forces, so Uncle Sam paid for him to go to college.

This guy had been a lieutenant in Vietnam.

He told me they had a high mortality rate among lieutenants.

One of the main reasons for this was 'fragging'.

Fragging wasn't enemy action.

It was your own troops.

What would happen is this.

A gung-ho lieutenant would arrive from the States.

He'd be desperate to prove himself, so he'd pick all the most dangerous missions for himself and his men.

Obviously the men didn't like this.

The troops were all enlisted and only had to survive their two-year stint.

They weren't going to do this by taking unnecessary risks.

So they would give him a warning.

When he pulled the blankets off his bed that night, there would be a fragmentation grenade lying there.

As this was only a warning, the pin would still be in it.

So it wouldn't explode.

Of course, if he ignored the warning, the next time it wouldn't have the pin in.

So the only thing stopping it exploding was the weight of the blanket.

And when he flipped the blanket back he, and the evidence, would disappear.

Of course, that only happened to lieutenants who didn't listen to the warning.

But it did happen.

That's the most important thing about warnings.

Don't make any that you aren't prepared to carry out.

Otherwise, the very first time you make a threat and don't follow through, everyone knows your threats are empty.

Far better to think first.

If you threaten something, are you really prepared to carry it out?

I watched one of my son's friends and his father once.

We were picking the two boys up from a bowling alley.

The boys asked us for some money to play the video games.

Both of us said the same thing.

'OK, here's £2 but that's it.'

Both the boys came back when they'd spent it.

The other son said, 'Dad, can I have some more?'

The father said, 'OK, another £2, but that's it.'

He went away and came back. 'Dad, can I have another £2?'

The father said, 'You've already had £4.'

The son said, 'Please.'

The father said, 'OK, but this is definitely the last.'

The son went away and came back for more.

The father gave him another £2 and said, 'This is the last time, I really mean it.'

When my son and I left it was still going on.

The father had trained the son to ignore what he said.

When he said no, it didn't mean no.

It meant pester me and I'll give in.

So that was their communication.

That's why in advertising account managers think all creatives are drama queens.

Constantly making threats they don't mean.

So it comes across as whining.

Threatening not to work on the account.

Threatening not to make changes to the script.

Threatening not to go on the shoot.

Threatening to let the account man edit the commercial himself.

Threatening to resign.

But they aren't going to do any of those things.

Everyone knows it.

So all they achieve is to train the account men to ignore them.

Isn't it better to only make threats you're prepared to carry out?

Like calling the client yourself, say.

Think first; would you do it?

If you would, then it's OK to threaten it.

Or leave and get another job.

Do you mean it?

If so, it's OK to threaten it.

That way everyone, including you, knows you mean what you say.

Like fragging.

One warning, then you carry out the threat.

Which is why the threat has power.

Imagine if the officer opened the covers on his bed and there was a fragmentation grenade with the pin in it.

Then the next night the same thing.

Then the next night the same thing.

After a week or so, it wouldn't even be a threat.

Just an irritation.

Someone has to know that when you say something, you mean it.

Otherwise don't say it.

Stir things up

Jane Juska was a retired schoolteacher.

One day she placed a small classified ad in the *New York Review of Books*.

It said, 'Before I turn 67, next March, I'd like to have lots of sex with a man I like. If you want to talk first, Trollope works for me.'

She got a lot of responses.

There are several clever and exciting things about what she did.

The medium she chose, for a start.

Not the back pages of any of the mags you'd normally find 'men-seeking-women' or 'women-seeking-men' ads.

It was placed in the *New York Review of Books*.

She was a retired English teacher.

She loved books, and reading.

She wanted sex, yes, but only with intelligent men who also loved literature.

So she let the search for intelligence dictate her media choice.

Not just the search for sex.

And, as a result, she stood out in that media much more than she would have elsewhere.

And that made her small classified ad unusual and daring.

Of course, what was really daring was deciding to do it in the first place.

Jane Juska was born in 1933.

She grew up in a world without the pill, television, mobile phones, rock and roll, or social media.

Women didn't even talk about things like sex.

So Jane grew up, got married, had a son and got divorced.

And, like all divorced women, that was supposed to be the end of her sex life.

For 30 years she worked as a schoolteacher.

Missing it occasionally, but accepting the inevitable.

Then she retired.

And it became obvious to her that, unless she did something about it, this was her future.

This was how her life would end.

She decided it was now or never.

And she did something to change that future.

She managed to combine her passions: love of literature, heterosexual intimacy and intelligent men.

After the ad ran she wrote a book about her experiences.

It's called *A Round-Heeled Woman* and it became an international bestseller.

And it transformed her life.

(The title refers to the Victorian description of 'a lady of easy virtue'.

A woman who would lie on her back so quickly her shoes
must have round heels.)
When Jane Juska placed the ad she didn't know where it
would all lead.
She just knew you only get one life.
And she had one last chance: use it or lose it.
She knew she had to disrupt things.
She had to disrupt the inevitability of a future she didn't
want.
We talk a lot about disruption in advertising.
But we don't really do much of it.
Not really.
We just do something slightly different.
Nothing we can't predict the outcome of.
What stops us being more daring is our fear of other people's
opinions.
Our client, our peers, our boss, consumers, even *Campaign*.
But, as Jane Juska found out, public opinion doesn't really
exist.
We just think it does.
Sure, some people were disgusted by what she did.
There will always be people like that.
But many more were curious and intrigued by what she did.
Many women wrote to thank her.

After they read her book they realized they weren't the only people in that situation.

This gave them the courage to transform their own lives.

To live before they died.

I think what she did is a great lesson.

Not just about sex.

But about facing the fear of whatever stops us.

Usually that fear is what we think other people will think.

We can't be successful and confident if we try to live life with no risk.

We can't be disruptive if we constantly seek permission.

Imagine if Jane Juska had asked everyone their opinion before she did it.

What answer do you think she would have got?

No.

So she wouldn't have done it.

Because no one can see anything truly disruptive being successful before it's done.

Only afterwards.

And, when it's successful, everyone agrees it was a good idea.

Because it worked.

So our life, and our work, will be as exciting as we make it.

And actually, the only person we have to worry about is ourself.

That's whose opinion is stopping us.

If we can learn to ignore ourselves, we can do anything we want.

Trust

Tony Adams was the captain of Arsenal, and one of the best defenders they ever had.

When he controlled their defence it was the best in the Premiership.

A couple of years ago I read his book.

It wasn't a good book.

Sports biographies hardly ever are.

But there's usually something you can learn, somewhere in there.

A simple principle.

And there was in Tony Adams' book.

I don't remember the exact words, but it was something like this.

'I wouldn't try to take the ball off the opposing forward.

See, if I went to take the ball I was committed.

And, if I missed, he could just go past me.

Plus there's the possibility of missing the ball and getting the player.

In which case I'd give away a free kick in a dangerous area.

So I never tried to take the ball off them.

I'd just shut them down.

Stay right on them and let them know they weren't getting past me.

I'd do this about 30 yards out.

They knew they weren't getting past me, but they knew I wouldn't take the ball.

This meant they had a chance to shoot, which is irresistible for most forwards.

So that's what they'd do, shoot from 30 yards.

And I knew I had David Seaman behind me.

And I knew he could handle pretty much anything from 30 yards.'

This is a man speaking who really knows his defence.

He knows his teammates.

So he knows who he can trust.

He's not playing like an individual but as part of a team.

He knows exactly how the different parts operate.

And what his job in the machine is.

And the machine works if everyone does their job as well as they can.

Instead of watching what someone else is doing.

That's how I like to work.

With different people each being responsible for different jobs.

Everyone fitting in and doing their specialist part.

Of course, everyone's got an opinion about everyone else's job.

And you make that available as input.

But whoever is responsible for their area needs to be responsible.

Not spend half their time worrying about someone else's area.

You have to find out who you can trust to do what.

Then, when you know that, trust them.

Don't keep trying to do their job.

Feeling you have to take the ball off an attacker is only necessary when you don't trust the goalie.

If you trust the goalie to handle long-range shots, make sure that's what he gets.

I'm the same when I work with a new account man.

When they're first presenting work to the client I go along with them.

If they do it better than me I know I don't need to go again.

I know I can trust them.

It's the same with art directors.

Gordon Smith, my partner for decades, has a better visual sense than me.

And like all the best art directors, he's a fusspot about detail. I'm not.

So I don't go on stills shoots, or to retouching, or grading commercials.

I trust him.

Planners, TV producers, media guys, whatever their job.

I like to know what they do.

And if they can do their job better than I could.

Then if it goes wrong, I can't bitch about it.

Because I couldn't have done it better.

So I can concentrate on just doing my job 100%.

Generally I like Tony Adams' approach.

Find out who you're working with and what they're good at.

Find out what you can trust them to do.

Then trust them.

Having some skin in the game

Max Forsythe is a photographer.

He was telling me about the time he flew from Israel to Cairo, on El Al.

He went to the airport to check in.

A young woman checked his luggage.

She was very thorough, but Max expected that.

Israel knows it's surrounded by hostile states.

Being wary of terrorist bombs is almost second nature.

And so she was perfectly pleasant, friendly and chatty, as she went through his luggage.

When she'd finished, Max said goodbye.

The young woman said, 'Oh, I'll see you on board.'

Max said, 'Are you flying to Cairo?'

She said, 'I have to, it's El Al policy.'

Max said, 'Why? Do you live in Cairo?'

She said, 'No, I live here, in Israel.'

Max said, 'How come you're flying to Cairo?'

She said, 'Standard El Al procedure. If you check the passengers' luggage, you have to fly on the plane.'

How about that?

The person who inspects the passengers' luggage for bombs has to bet their life on how well they do their job.

That'll concentrate your mind.

Imagine if we had to do our jobs like that.

Like it was really, really important to us.

As they say in New York, 'Having some skin in the game'.

Maybe not our life, that would be silly.

But how about our house?

If we had to bet our house on our decisions, would we make the same decisions?

Would we make them the same way?

Would creatives be fighting for the latest esoteric/trendy technique just so they could win an award?

Knowing that if the ordinary consumers didn't understand the ad they'd lose their house?

Would planners be recommending changing the advertising based on what a couple of focus groups said?

Knowing they were betting their mortgage on the result?

Would account men be willing to change whatever the client wanted to change, just to keep them happy?

Knowing they were betting their house on the client's whim?

Would clients be quite so eager to get their own way, just because they could?

Even if getting their own way might cost them their house?

Or would everyone take their decisions a bit more seriously?

Would they weigh all the implications before they acted?

Would they carefully consider everyone else's point of view?

Put their ego aside.

Look at everything from every possible angle.

Make sure nothing is left to chance.

Instead of just getting their own way.

Of course, everyone has some skin in the game.

People can lose their jobs.

But you can get another job.

Unlike at El Al, no one bets their life.

Which is the reason why El Al has a reputation as the safest airline to fly with if you're worried about terrorist bombs.

The difference between involvement and commitment

There's a difference between involvement and commitment.

If we're merely 'involved' in something then we don't have to give it our all.

If it fails, it's not the end of the world.

But if we're 'committed' that's a different matter.

Then it really is do or die.

We've got a lot more at stake.

It's very important to know the difference.

And be honest with ourselves.

There's a saying in New York about the difference between involvement and commitment.

They say it's like ham and eggs.

The chicken is involved, but the pig is committed.

Many Americans see that as the problem with Europeans.

They're only involved, never committed.

So they can't be relied on.

In 1940 that was a huge problem.

Britain stood alone against Germany and needed American help.

But the Americans saw Britain as weak and about to crumble.

Some people in Britain even wanted to make peace with the Germans.

The USA didn't see the British as committed enough to make a reliable ally.

But all that changed, during the course of what the French still see as the most shameful act of treachery in Franco-British history.

The French had already surrendered to Germany.

Their main ships were at port in Mers-el-Kebir, in North Africa.

Some of the most modern, most powerful battleships in the world.

If they fell into German hands, they could be used to cut the Atlantic convoys.

Then Britain would be defeated.

Obviously, Churchill couldn't allow that.

So he sent a British fleet to Mers-el-Kebir.

They waited outside the port and issued the French fleet with an ultimatum.

This is the gist of it:

'You have 3 choices:

1) You can either sail your ships with us and fight against Germany.

2) We can escort your ships to a neutral port, like the USA, where they must stay for the rest of the war.

3) Or you can scuttle your ships where they are, right now.

You have six hours to decide.'

The French said they would do none of these things.

So, when the six-hour deadline was up, the Royal Navy sank the French fleet.

Right where it was moored, in the harbour, virtually defenceless.

Killing several thousand French sailors.

The French have never forgiven us.

Churchill said it was the one decision he was most ashamed of.

But the Americans finally decided to give us the aid we needed.

Because it was apparent to everyone.

Now we were no longer just involved.

Now we were committed.

Now there was no going back.

Determination is very important to Americans.

And finally they saw we were determined enough to win.

We had staked everything.

We didn't hold anything back.

Commitment is a very difficult thing for English people.

It's uncool for a start.

We're never supposed to look as if we're trying too hard.

What if we give everything we've got and we still lose?

We won't have any excuses.

At least if we don't give everything, we can say we're not that bothered.

We didn't really try.

As Ricky Ponting said about cricket, 'When Australia loses we look for things we can change.

When England loses you look for excuses.'

It's the same with war, with sport, with business, with relationships.

And it's the same in what we do.

If we commit too much to work, we're a workaholic.

Almost as if we've got a problem.

As if there's something wrong with actually wanting to work.

When we could be over the pub.

Or at home watching TV.

Or reading, or at the gym, or sleeping.

Or anything, so long as it isn't work.

Because being involved is OK, but being 'committed' is seen as somehow unhealthy.

Too extreme.

Funny thing, though.

All the people who are really successful aren't just involved. They're committed.

Strategy is what. Tactics is how

The Second World War was really a story of two people.

Adolf Hitler and Winston Churchill.

Pretty much everything that went right and wrong can be
traced back to how they did their jobs.

Put simply, Churchill was a strategist.

Hitler was a tactician who thought he was a strategist.

Strategy is the big picture.

Tactics are the little pictures that make up the big picture.

Tacticians are specialists.

Strategists are generalists.

The strategist oversees a lot of tacticians.

He tells them what he wants done.

But he doesn't tell them how to do it.

He operates what management experts call 'tight targets,
loose controls'.

That's the proper way for a strategist to behave.

That's how Churchill behaved.

In other words, give the tacticians a job and let them get on
with it.

That's what a strategist does.

But Hitler wasn't a strategist.

He was a tactician who thought he was a strategist.

So he didn't really have a big picture to concentrate on.

Because he didn't have a big picture, he kept interfering in tactics.

Every general and every admiral had to get every decision approved by Hitler before they could make a move.

This meant Hitler would often change tactics while the generals were in the middle of executing them.

He had no concept of the logistics of moving an army.

So he moved them at will, and ignored the advice of the experts.

He had no strategy above winning battles.

So Germany had no strategic leader, and a bad tactician overruling the experts.

Churchill, on the other hand, had a big, simple strategy.

Get America into the war.

The biggest, most powerful country on the planet.

He didn't have time to overrule his generals, or even discuss tactics.

Tactics were their job, not his.

He would give them a target: 'I need a victory in North Africa. No excuses.'

Then he'd leave them to it.

If they couldn't deliver, he'd fire them and get another general.

Meanwhile, because he wasn't interfering with tactics,

Churchill was free to spend all his time working on his strategy.

Criss-crossing the Atlantic to meet with Roosevelt and address the government in Washington.

To concentrate on changing American public opinion.

He knew, once America was in the war, it was only a matter of time until Germany was beaten.

While Churchill pursued his single-minded strategy, Hitler, without a strategy, made the biggest blunder of the war.

He invaded Russia.

After the Battle of Britain he realized we weren't going to surrender, so he got bored and attacked someone else instead.

And while his generals were moving their armies to attack in the north, Hitler changed his mind.

He told them to attack in the south.

And while they were getting 2 million men to change direction, he changed his mind again.

And decided maybe they should attack in the north after all.

And the armies wasted weeks and weeks going back and forth.

And by that time it had started snowing.

And we all know how that story ended.

Russia destroyed the German army and America came in on Britain's side.

Strategists 1 – Tacticians 0.

Personally, I'm not a strategist, I'm a tactician.

The good thing is I know I'm a tactician.

I don't try to do strategy.

And I like to work with strategists who don't try to do tactics.

I like a CEO, or MD, or a client, who does the strategy.

They tell me what they want, and they let me do it.

If I can't do it, they get someone else.

But they don't try to do my job.

They do the strategy, they let me do the tactics.

When it's worked best for me (with partners or with clients),
that's how it's worked.

Firm targets, loose controls.

The best strategists do the 'what' and let the tacticians do
the 'how'.

When strength becomes weakness

I mentioned earlier that when I was at art school in New York,
I knew a guy who had served in Vietnam.

He'd been a captain in the artillery, and his main job was
guarding the DMZ.

The DMZ was the De-Militarized Zone: the strip of land
between the North and South that was no man's land.

No one was supposed to be there, and anyone who was, was
killed.

He said the main weapon they used was called Lazy Dog.

Lazy Dog was an artillery shell: a massive amount of
explosive, around which was packed millions of needles.

Lazy Dog would burst in the air over the target.

Then anything underneath was shredded as if it had been put
in a blender.

He said the entire DMZ had listening devices planted in the
ground.

Whenever they heard a noise, they fired off a few Lazy Dogs.

Next day they'd go out and investigate.

Most of the time all they'd find was some blood and fur.

Because it had usually just been an animal rooting around.

I said it didn't sound a very effective way to spend millions of
dollars fighting a war.

He agreed.

He said it was the weakness of the US military that they couldn't do anything without vast amounts of technology.

He said the Vietcong knew that.

As long as US soldiers had access to their expensive technology, they'd be superior.

But if they could get to them without their technology, they could beat them.

He asked me if I knew the Vietcong 'rule of thumb' for shooting down helicopters.

I said I didn't.

He said, 'Shooting something with small-arms fire just depends on how far away it is.

In the US Army we have complicated range-finding technology to tell us if something is close enough to hit.

The Vietcong don't have any of that stuff.

When they hear a helicopter they look up, stretch their arm out and hold their thumb over it.

If the chopper is bigger than their thumb, it's close enough to shoot down with pretty much anything.

If the helicopter is smaller than their thumb, it's too far away.'

How brilliant is that?

Range-finding technology that the simplest peasant can carry in their head.

So there you have two views of technology.

On the one hand we can spend millions upon millions of

dollars doing something that makes us feel reassured, but is totally ineffective.

Just because we have a belief that technology must always be superior.

As long as we've got the newest, most expensive, most complicated technology.

On the other hand we can spend no money at all.

We can use what's around, combined with a great idea, to do something really effective.

An idea so good it will go viral among the entire population of a country.

Even without any Internet or a single computer.

Can you see any parallels with the world we work in?

On the one hand we can worship technology for itself.

We can believe in it like a religion.

We can trust that it's always the answer to every question.

Then our strength becomes our weakness.

On the other hand we start from the point of having a great idea.

Then use technology to propagate that idea.

When and where it's relevant, according to the job that needs doing.

Because technology is a tool.

And, like any tool, we can hold it by either the handle or the blade.

God is in the detail

Jackie Stewart was Formula One world champion three times.

People say what made him a great driver was that he was better in the rain than anyone else.

The other Formula One drivers knew that, unlike them, he actually enjoyed driving in it.

The wetter, the better.

So they knew however fast Jackie Stewart was going was the absolute limit.

And they backed off.

They knew they couldn't pass him in the rain because he loved it.

That was a big factor in him winning three World Championships.

After he retired, I read an interview with him.

He said he actually hated driving in the rain.

It was a myth that he invented and kept going.

Because he knew all the other drivers hated it and feared it, too.

So he saw a way to take advantage.

If he made everyone think he loved it, they wouldn't try to overtake him.

Jackie Stewart didn't win three World Championships just by being the fastest driver.

He won by being the smartest driver.

His motto was, 'In order to finish first, first you have to finish.'

He criticized flashier drivers who would get their cars to skid around corners.

Sure, it pleased the crowd and looked good.

But it scrubbed valuable rubber off the tyres.

Rubber that might mean a pit stop to change them.

A pit stop that might cost ten seconds.

Ten seconds that might be the difference between first place and nowhere.

Jackie Stewart nursed his car round the track, making sure he did as little damage to it as possible.

Because if any part of the car broke, the driver didn't finish the race.

And if he didn't finish he couldn't win.

Jackie Stewart didn't even drive himself around on ordinary roads.

He had a chauffeur.

He'd seen other racing drivers take their skills onto ordinary roads.

And get killed racing with other drivers.

Because ordinary roads are more dangerous than race tracks.

On a race track everyone is going the same way.

On a race track everyone is a professional.

Everyone knows what everyone else is expected to do.

Ordinary roads aren't like that.

Mike Hawthorn was a world champion before Jackie Stewart.

He got killed overtaking near Brighton.

He ran head-on into a car coming the other way.

You don't get cars coming the other way on a race track.

So Jackie Stewart didn't drive on ordinary roads.

He wasn't paid to.

The chauffeur was the professional at driving on ordinary roads.

It was his job to get him safely to the race track.

Where, in one drive, he'd earn many times what he paid the chauffeur.

Jackie Stewart was a careful, thoughtful man.

Everywhere he raced he even took his own doctor, and equipment, along.

In case he crashed, he wanted someone on the spot.

He'd seen too many drivers die on the way to hospital.

And he put a lot of thought into what sort of doctor to take.

He said, 'I didn't take a surgeon, that would have made no sense. He couldn't operate on the side of the race track.

I took an anaesthetist. Someone who could keep whatever was left of me alive, until I got to hospital.'

Jackie Stewart always said that what gave him a head start over other drivers was that he was dyslexic.

No one knew about dyslexia when he was young.

So everyone just thought he was stupid.

This meant that if he was going to beat anyone else, he'd have to try much, much harder.

He'd have to pay more attention, leave nothing to chance.

He would have to concentrate on every single detail, everywhere.

If he couldn't compete by being smarter, he'd compete with more effort.

This meant every single thing, no matter how small, was an opportunity.

A way to gain an advantage.

He even used senses other people ignored.

All drivers used their sight, and hearing, and sense of touch.

Jackie Stewart even used his sense of smell.

At one particular race, coming into a fast corner, he smelt new mown grass.

He backed off the accelerator and rounded the corner to find a car had ploughed off the road and onto the grass bank.

He drove round the oil and debris and carried on.

Several other drivers didn't notice the smell of grass.

Or at least, they didn't pay any attention.

Either way they crashed, or skidded out of the race.

And Jackie Stewart won.

Any detail you don't pay attention to, is somewhere you could lose.

Any detail you do pay attention to, is somewhere you could win.

PART EIGHT

FORM FOLLOWS FUNCTION

One man's fish is another man's poisson

A few years ago, I went back to Barking, in east London, to
visit my mum.

While we were having a cup of tea she said to me, 'Isn't it a
shame, that nice young boy over the road's been locked up for
robbery?'

I said, 'What did he do, Mum?'

She showed me the local paper.

She said, 'It's in here. It says he robbed a bank. I don't know
about that. He was always very nice and polite to me. Always
said, "Hello, Mrs Trott," and helped me across the road with
my shopping.'

I read the report of the trial in the paper and, sure enough,
he'd held up a bank with a sawn-off shotgun.

But the part that interested me was what his dad had to say.

He told the reporter, 'They'd better lock the little sod up, if I
get hold of him I'll kill him. That shotgun cost me nearly a
grand and he's sawn the bleeding barrels off.'

I found that fascinating.

Someone found great beauty and value in something.

But to someone else it was just an object to be used.

No big deal.

To his dad it was a finely engraved, beautifully balanced piece
of craftsmanship to be lovingly polished and oiled.

To the son it was a tool to do a job.

But it wasn't quite right for the job he wanted, so he fixed it.

The barrels were getting in the way, so he cut them off.

There, that's better.

Now he could carry it under his coat.

In his terms he fixed it, in his dad's terms he ruined it.

The beautifully engraved barrels were lying on the floor of the shed in a pile of metal filings.

It reminded me of something I had read a couple of years back.

Someone bought a house in East Yorkshire and they were renovating it, clearing out the old junk.

There was a tatty old roller blind over the kitchen window, covered in grease.

As they were chucking it in the skip they noticed it had something scrawled all over it.

They unrolled it and found five original David Hockney drawings on it.

The blind was eventually sold for a fortune at auction.

It will form the centrepiece of the Museum of Modern and Contemporary Art in Cumbria.

Thousands of people will pay to come and stand in front of it and look at it.

They won't be able to touch it because it's too precious.

But to someone else, all it was good for was to make a blind for the kitchen window.

Do you ever get that feeling about your work?

People don't appreciate what you're trying to do.

The job you're doing isn't the job they want.

Jim Kelly (founder of RKCR, Y&R) once told me about what he called the 'Procter & Gamble triangle'.

It goes like this.

The account man shows the P&G client the idea: a triangle.

The client says, 'That's great, we like the triangle idea. But we think it could be better.'

Then they cut the triangle in half down the middle.

They say, 'We like the left-hand side just where it is. But we think the right-hand side would be better upside down and moved to the left, like this.'

Then they move the other half across so the two halves now form a square.

The account man says, 'But that's not a triangle any more, now it's a square.'

They say, 'What do you mean? We haven't taken anything away. We haven't added anything. We've just rearranged it. It's still the basic triangle idea you showed us.'

The account man says, 'But it isn't a triangle any more, it's a square now.'

They say, 'Don't be silly. It's still exactly the same idea you showed us, a triangle. It's still got all the elements. All we've done is make it better.'

The truth is, no one's really happy.

Neither side has got what they really want.

Because either the brief has changed, or it's the wrong solution.

That's why they're adapting something to do a job it was never intended for.

They should have started off with a brief for a square.

Then the client would have been shown a square.

Rather than try to adapt a triangle to be a square.

I went to a Bauhaus art school in New York.

So the mantra was 'form follows function'.

Get the brief for the function right in the first place.

Then the form comes out of the function.

Don't change the form to suit a different function.

Don't go to Purdey's for a sawn-off shotgun.

Don't use a Hockney for a roller blind.

Chance favours the connected mind

I've just seen a great TED talk by Steven Johnson, the bestselling author.

In it he makes the point that ideas usually aren't 'Eureka' moments.

Someone very rarely goes off alone and has a sudden flash of insight.

More usually it's a team game.

It happens in a more crowded environment.

With people talking and swapping ideas.

Someone raises a problem.

Someone suggests a solution.

Someone shoots it down.

Someone finds a way round the objection.

Someone refines the idea.

Everyone thinks about that.

Eventually everyone agrees it's a good idea.

And off you go.

Great ideas don't come out of limbo.

They come as solutions to problems.

He gives a great example.

Timothy Prestero runs a company called Design that Matters.

This is a company staffed entirely by volunteers.

Its mission is to use design to help create a better life for people in the Third World.

One of the main problems is infant mortality.

A million premature babies die each year because they don't have incubators.

A neonatal incubator is a sophisticated piece of technology costing around $40,000.

The main problem is: what happens when it goes wrong?

No one knows how to fix it.

Figures show that 98% of the incubators that break down never get repaired.

So that defined the problem.

How to build an incubator that people in the Third World could repair.

As always, the start point is to investigate the brief.

So they went to rural communities to see what skills were available.

Obviously there was little or no technology.

No microwave ovens, no DVD players, no computers, no dishwashers, no washing machines, no fridges.

But there was one thing that every community seemed to have.

Pick-up trucks.

Four-wheel drives.

Vans.

They all seemed to have vehicles of some sort.

And because these vehicles were precious, they looked after them.

They knew how to keep them going.

Every local community knew how to repair cars and trucks.

So the answer was obvious.

Not easy, but obvious.

Design an incubator that's made from car parts.

That way, when it breaks down, the local mechanic can fix it.

And that's what Timothy Prestero's team did.

The incubator they designed looks exactly like the neonatal incubators you see in our hospitals.

But under the mattress it has two sealed-beam headlamps.

These provide heat by warming the baby's mattress, and by warming the air around the baby.

The incubator has an automobile air-filtration system to clean the baby's air.

It has a ventilation fan to circulate the clean air around the baby.

It has a car reversing-alarm and indicator lights for warning signals, in case anything goes wrong.

It runs off its own 12-volt car battery.

It also has a car recharger in the base.

And it has small, inflatable wheels that can be mended at any cycle repair shop.

So any rural mechanic can fix this incubator if it breaks down.

For me that's how you analyse a problem.

That's how you define the brief.

Gathering information.

Working together.

Opening things out, not closing things down.

That's how it should be.

That's form following function.

And right now that car-parts incubator is saving little babies' lives.

Come off broadcast, go on receive

A few years back the Ministry of Defence ordered a new radio system.

The radios would be used by ships, helicopters, planes, tanks and infantry.

Involved in the procurement process were specialists from the army, navy and air force.

Everyone had their own particular demands.

And each was adamant their concerns were the priority.

There was much wrangling and thumping of desks.

During the procurement process they were told the radios could be fitted with a GPS tracking device.

It would take a bit longer but they'd always be able to locate exactly where each radio was.

All the specialists agreed they didn't need a GPS tracking device.

And they didn't have time to wait while a GPS tracking device was fitted.

They must have the new radios now.

So the new state-of-the-art system was produced to their joint specifications and rushed into service.

It's been in use for a while now, and it's been quite successful.

Just one problem.

Around 4,000 radios have gone missing.

That's around 10% of the total number the forces were issued with.

No one knows where they are.

Does the Taliban have them, can they listen to our troops?

Are the radios being sold to foreign powers?

Can they hack into all our military communications?

The system cost £2.4 billion.

48,000 radios were issued.

Along with 30,000 computer terminals and 30,000 platforms.

And 75,000 personnel trained to use them.

And we don't know if it's all useless.

Because we don't know where one in ten radios are, or who has them.

Of course, if they'd put a GPS tracking device in the radios we'd know the exact location of every single one.

But the specialists in charge of procurement didn't believe it was necessary.

So it wasn't considered important.

And now the entire system may be useless because of it.

Because of specialists thinking that their area is the only really important area.

Specialists who can't see the bigger picture.

We're all guilty of that.

We're all specialists who believe our area is the most important.

And we fight to make our concerns the priority.

Planners believe as long as the ad answers the strategy, that's all that matters.

Creatives believe as long as the ad wins an award, that's all that matters.

Account men believe as long as the account is profitable, that's all that matters.

And clients and media have their agendas, too.

Everyone believes their bit is the most important.

Each fighting for priority.

And no one is standing back and looking at the big picture.

Wrong brief = wrong solution

The narrowest strip of land between North and South
America is Panama.

It's only about 50 miles wide.

But it's wide enough to separate the Atlantic and the Pacific
oceans.

For ships, this used to mean sailing thousands of miles south.

Then through the terrible storms at Cape Horn.

Then thousands of miles north again.

Obviously it made sense to dig a canal across this strip of
land.

The French didn't see it as a problem.

Especially as they'd just built a canal twice that long through
Egypt.

The Suez Canal.

They thought if this was half as long, it should be half as
difficult.

And in 1880, Ferdinand de Lesseps began building.

But it wasn't half as difficult.

It was much, much more difficult.

Men began dying from malaria, a problem they hadn't had in
Egypt.

Because Egypt is a desert, whereas Panama is a jungle.

So there were many, many more insects everywhere.

Since insects were obviously the source of malaria, the brief was also obvious.

Stop them crawling onto the beds and biting people.

The solution was ingenious.

Insects can't crawl across water, so use it as a barrier.

So they dug trenches around their tents and huts, and filled them with water.

And in the hospitals they placed a saucer of water under the legs of each of the beds.

And it worked.

Every morning the saucers and the trenches would be full of dead insects.

So why were people still dying of malaria?

It made no sense.

The brief was to stop the insects crawling into the beds and tents.

They'd done that.

If malaria wasn't coming from the insects, how could they fight it?

The answer was, they couldn't.

The French were forced to abandon plans to build the canal.

In 1893, after 13 years, and 22,000 dead, they went home.

What the French hadn't allowed for was that their brief was wrong.

It was true that insects were the source of malaria.

But not the insects that crawled.

The insects that flew.

Mosquitoes.

They didn't drown in the water in the saucers and trenches.

In fact the mosquitoes would breed in standing water.

Which is exactly what the trenches and saucers provided.

So not only did they not solve the problem, they made it worse.

The French hadn't questioned the brief.

And when it didn't work, they gave up.

The Americans had a different attitude.

To them, a brief isn't sacrosanct.

If the answer doesn't work, maybe the brief is wrong.

So they came up with a different brief.

Not to solve the problem of crawling insects.

To solve the problem of mosquitoes.

In 1904 they started work.

But not on the canal.

First they started work on the mosquitoes.

They made sure all pools of standing water within 200 yards of their camps were drained.

Where they couldn't be drained, oil was poured into them.

Where oil wasn't enough, carbolic acid and caustic soda were poured into them.

They killed every mosquito anywhere near the canal.

And, just to make sure, all buildings and all beds were screened.

So none could possibly fly in while people slept.

They finished building the Panama Canal in 1914.

Two years ahead of schedule.

It took the Americans 10 years to totally complete the job.

It took the French 13 years to fail and give up.

What was the difference?

You can't get the right solution if you've got the wrong brief.

The difference between efficiency and effectiveness

My dad was a real old-fashioned copper.

In the days when they used to ride around on bikes,

One day he was riding past some road works.

A steamroller was going up and down over the hot tar they'd just laid.

Another bloke was riding his bike past the same road works.

For some reason the bloke fell off his bike.

And in trying to avoid the hot tar he nearly rolled under the steamroller.

He only just managed to escape being squashed flat.

But the steamroller did just catch the edge of his leg.

It ran along the length of his thigh.

The skin was stretched so tight, the thigh split open, from the hip to the knee.

The pain must have been excruciating.

The man screamed and passed out.

By the time Dad got off his bike, the man was unconscious and choking.

Swallowing his tongue.

All the flesh on his thigh was laid open, flat on the ground.

The exposed thigh bone was lying on top of it.

So, in that situation, what's the first thing you do?

Dad thought the first thing to do was keep the bloke alive.

Currently he was choking to death.

He was swallowing his tongue.

So dad took out his penknife and pulled the bloke's tongue out as far as he could.

Then he stuck the penknife through the tongue.

Now the bloke couldn't swallow it.

Right, next thing, stop the loss of blood and try to save the leg.

So he asked if someone could get him some safety pins and string, quick.

One lady rushed inside her house and brought some back.

Then dad cleaned as much gravel as he could away from the open flesh.

And he wrapped the flesh back around the bone.

Then with a mixture of safety pins and string, he stuck it all tightly back together.

I asked dad what happened to the bloke.

Dad said he saw him around a few times afterwards and he was fine.

His tongue was probably sore for a bit, and his leg probably wasn't as pretty as it had been.

But he was alive and he had both legs.

If Dad had worried about not cutting the bloke's tongue.

If he'd worried about giving him a scar on the leg.

If he'd been unsure or dithered, the bloke wouldn't be alive or walking around.

So, instead of worrying about the finer details, Dad got the important bit right.

Now contrast that with the way we do our jobs.

Do we get our priorities right?

What would have happened if Dad had done his job the way we do ours?

First off, he wouldn't have touched the bloke until an independent research consultancy had made a thorough evaluation.

They'd have needed to recruit some focus groups of leg-users and ask their opinion.

Then they'd have needed to review the results.

Eventually they'd have debriefed Dad on their findings.

They'd have told him that basically there was a fundamental problem with the leg.

And that there were several possible ways to approach this.

They'd suggest some 'ideation workshops'.

Afterwards they'd present a range of possible approaches.

Eventually, everyone would agree on the preferred solution.

The strategy would be to repair the leg and reuse it if possible.

So that's the brief they'd give to the creative department.

In time, the creative department would come back with a beautiful idea of a leg.

This would then be researched among different groups of leg-users.

The leg-users would all have comments and opinions.

So the original idea would have to be changed and refined.

They'd agree to make the toenails shorter, to have less hair, to make the calf more shapely.

When it's finally agreed, they'd get a quote from a production company.

The best in the field, so obviously they'd be very expensive.

But this will be the perfect leg.

So now everyone concentrates on the details.

Getting the skin-colour perfect, the exact shape of the knees, the ankles.

And finally the leg is finished.

Ready to be walked on.

Just one small problem.

The man died six weeks ago.

Somewhere, everyone got their priorities wrong.

Everyone was so concerned with getting every detail exactly perfect.

They forgot the purpose of what they were doing.

They were so concerned with the 'form', they forgot the 'function'.

They were so fixated on the execution, they forgot the idea.

They were so worried about being efficient, they forgot about being effective.

I once heard the difference between 'efficiency' and 'effectiveness' defined as follows:
'Efficiency is doing things right. Effectiveness is doing the right things.'

PART NINE

THE HUMAN MIND IS OUR MEDIUM

Game-changing thinking

Nearly 100 years ago, Herman Hesse wrote *Steppenwolf*.

At the end, the main character gets a chance to go back and live his life over.

To do all the things he wishes he'd done.

To take the chances he missed.

We'd all like a chance to go back and do things right.

We wonder what life would have been if we'd done things even slightly differently.

What if we hadn't simply walked by that pretty girl?

What if we'd stopped and said hello?

What if we'd made that phone call, taken that job offer, or spoken up in that meeting?

What would our life have been like?

It's a question that fascinates us.

Imagine if we could tap into those feelings for advertising.

When I was on a D&AD jury judging the Black Pencil awards, I saw a campaign I'd never seen before.

It's for Gatorade and it does just that.

It gets to answer the question that bugs us all.

What if?

The strange thing is, what I saw wasn't even advertising.

It was an idea to trigger a bigger idea.

That's what I really loved about it.

It was bigger than advertising.

The video I saw explained that in the late nineties there was an ice hockey match between two high schools.

This was a match full of intense passion and rivalry.

The game was tied.

Suddenly one player was tackled.

He went down and a skate ran across his neck.

It severed his jugular vein.

His uniform, the other players, the ice, were covered in blood.

Everyone thought he was dead.

But they got him to hospital and saved his life, and eventually he recovered fully.

Obviously the game had to be called off.

And 15 years later the locals still argue about who would have won.

So Gatorade gave the exact same players the chance to replay that game.

These are men now in their mid-thirties.

Sure, they were out of condition, overweight, sedentary.

But so was everyone on the other team.

Gatorade gave them all three months to train for the rematch.

They gave them professional athletic trainers and medical supervision.

The guys really found out how out of shape they were.

As they trained they got dizzy, they got cramp, they threw up.

But eventually they got back into shape.

One guy lost 56 lbs (4 stone) for the replay.

This game touched something in American sports fans.

People wanted to replay basketball games, baseball games,

American football games.

It became something everyone wanted to be part of.

It even became a reality TV series.

Cameras would watch the teams training each week.

And the best thing was how it all worked for Gatorade.

A sport drink that helps replace the energy you've lost.

Isn't that a great natural fit?

You're mid-thirties.

You've lost a lot of the energy you had when you were 18.

No problem, Gatorade can help replace lost energy.

I didn't even see any commercials for this campaign.

That's what I liked so much about it.

The idea was bigger than just commercials.

It tapped into a really deep truth about everyone.

Who wouldn't like to have more energy?

How can we talk about that in a way that's unique to

Gatorade?

That wasn't standard advertising thinking.

It wasn't even a better kind of advertising thinking.

Gatorade wasn't just playing the same game better.

They were changing the game.

The train is leaving the station

My wife is an art director.

Recently she went to the Marketing Forum.

Being a creative, she expected to be bored by lots of case
histories, graphs, charts, numbers.

But one client told an amazingly creative story about the
birth of a brand.

It started when he was working in Belgium.

Every day he had to try to sell margarine to people who
didn't want it.

It was dispiriting work.

To cheer himself up, every day he went to the same pastry
shop and ate a delicious chocolate pastry.

Eventually it became clear to him.

'I don't like margarine.

I do like chocolate.

I'm in the wrong game.'

Doing what you love is always the best idea.

So he quit his job and began working on perfecting a
delicious, rich chocolate pudding.

He worked on it until he had it exactly right.

Now he needed marketing.

He needed a positioning, a name, packaging – a brand,
in fact.

So he went to see an agency and asked if they could do that for him.

They said, 'Leave it with us.'

So he waited.

And he waited.

Three weeks later they hadn't contacted him, so he called them.

They said, 'We-ell ... You'd better come in, we've got something to show you.'

He went to see them.

They said, 'We've got some bad news, we're afraid. It looks like someone else has already done it.'

His jaw dropped.

They said, 'Yes, unfortunately, virtually the same product, same positioning, everything. We've managed to get hold of some pictures.

If you promise not to let it leave this room, we'll show you.'

He nodded.

They said, 'You wanted a stylish, classy chocolate pudding, deliciously gooey, yet premium? Look, theirs is called Gü.

It's got the German umlaut (two little dots) over the letter u, so it looks like a smiley face.

And it rhymes with "goo", so it's fun, but classy.

A bit like Häagen-Dazs.'

The client's face fell.

He said, 'I can't believe it. That's a great name.'

They said, 'Yes, and look at the packaging: it's dark, rich, elegant. Indulgent and chocolatey, but also stylish.'

The client said, 'This is terrible. How advanced are they?'

They said, 'Their sales force is ready to start selling it in. We're worried because we think they'll be very successful.'

The client said, 'What do you mean, you think they'll be successful? Of course they'll be successful. It's a brilliant product, a brilliant name, a brilliant pack design. It's exactly what I wanted, dammit.'

And he sat back, depressed, thinking about all the success he could have had if only he'd had that idea first.

Then the account man smiled and said, 'Well, if you really mean that, I may have some good news for you.'

The client said, 'What?'

The account man said, 'I made that story up. No one has actually done anything.

This is our presentation to you: the name, the packaging, everything.

If you want it, you can have it.'

The client said he felt as if the sun had come out.

Instead of the usual shuffling and humming and hawing, he just took everything as it stood and went with it.

Isn't that great?

We never want anything so much as when we can't have it.

So instead of selling the client an idea in a way that lets him think he's got all the time in the world.

To fiddle with every tiny unimportant detail.

They let him see what's really important.

How will he feel if he sees a competitor has done it?

If he's been beaten to market?

He won't quibble about the serif on the typeface.

He won't worry that the background colour isn't exactly 100% perfect.

He'll just wish to God he'd done it.

What a great lesson.

Show the client the idea in a situation where he would give anything to have done it.

But it's too late, someone else got there first.

It's like a nightmare.

Then wake him up and tell him it was just a dream, and he's still got a chance to do it himself.

Instead of suspicion and hesitation, he'll feel gratitude and eagerness.

He'll be concentrating on the 95% that's right.

Not holding everything up for the tiny 5% that isn't.

We'll have a client who wants to move things forward, not hold things back.

By the way, the name of the client who told that story was James Averdieck.

And he's just sold that brand for £35 million.

Imagination vs reality

When my kids were young they liked to dress up for Halloween.

The usual thing: witches, vampires.

Lots of fake blood and pretend scars.

So we'd dress the basement up with the usual props.

Spider's webs everywhere, skeletons, monsters.

Try to make it look like a crypt or a graveyard.

The main idea being to make it as scary as possible.

Then we'd switch the lights off so it was pitch black, and give them a torch.

And leave them and their friends to tell ghost stories in the dark.

One year I thought I'd add to the atmosphere a bit.

So I went to HMV and bought a CD of horror movie sound effects.

Creaking coffin lids, groans, shrieks, axes chopping up bodies.

And I also bought a blank C120 cassette tape.

I wound the tape on until it was about halfway through.

Then I recorded a soft knocking sound from the CD.

Then silence.

Then more knocking, more insistent this time.

Silence.

Then a creaking coffin lid opening.

Then horrible groans.

More groans.

Then terrifying roars.

And finally screams.

Then I rewound the tape to the beginning.

And I put the cassette player in the corner of the basement, where no one could see it.

On Halloween, all the kids came down to the basement.

While they weren't looking, I turned the tape player on and left them alone.

For half an hour the children told scary ghost stories in the dark.

Each one trying to outdo the other in horror and gore.

While the tape player wound silently on over the blank bit.

Suddenly, the kids heard knocking coming from somewhere in the dark.

They stopped and looked.

Nothing.

Then, from the dark, the knocking got louder.

They froze.

Then the sound of a coffin lid creaking open.

They. Were. Terrified.

Then came the awful groan of a rotting corpse coming to life.

Suddenly the kids just jumped up and ran.

They were out of there like small rockets.

It took me a while to calm them down.

Eventually I convinced them to come back to the basement and showed them the tape player.

And eventually, they all laughed with relief.

And they understood the only really scary thing was their imagination.

But that's always true.

What we fear is nearly always worse than the reality.

And that's why sound can be more powerful than vision.

The power of suggestion over description.

To calm the kids down, we put a horror movie on the DVD player for them.

And they sat around watching it, eating popcorn.

Talking, joking and laughing.

And it wasn't nearly so scary as the basement.

Because that was just pictures.

And pictures are finite.

Whereas imagination is infinite.

Imagination is always as far as you can possibly go, plus one.

As Albert Einstein said, 'Imagination is more important than knowledge.

For knowledge is limited to all we now know and understand, while imagination embraces the entire world, and all there ever will be to know and understand.'

Just imagine

During the Second World War, my mum and sister were evacuated to Wales.

So my dad was living in the house on his own.

Because he was alone, he tended to go to bed early.

One night he was woken, about two in the morning.

By the sound of a piano playing.

Dad lay in bed for a minute, trying to work out what was happening.

Was the noise coming from inside or outside the house?

He knew they had an old upright piano in the front room.

But nobody used it.

And anyway, there wasn't anyone in the house.

So he got up and went to the top of the stairs and looked over.

He could definitely hear piano sounds coming from the front room, downstairs.

But the piano wasn't playing a tune.

Just a collection of weird, discordant notes.

So he started to go downstairs.

As he got closer he could hear a strange wailing noise.

High pitched, like a child in pain.

But not quite human.

He got to the bottom of the stairs and looked towards the living room.

Which was pitch black.

He put his head inside.

Nothing.

Except the jangling sounds coming from the piano.

And the high-pitched mournful wailing.

In the empty house.

In the dark.

At two in the morning.

The whole world was dead, except for this noise.

He walked over to the piano, and looked at the keys.

They were moving up and down.

Not in any order, just up and down.

And the echoey notes were playing.

And still, the high-pitched cries.

Then he opened the top of the piano and looked in.

A cat was walking up and down, inside the piano.

Trying to get out.

Crying in a high-pitched voice.

So dad reached in, grabbed the cat and put it outdoors.

Then he went back to bed and fell asleep.

See, as a policeman, it was his job to be rational in all situations.

Everything always had to have a logical explanation.

Personally, I don't think I'd even have gotten downstairs.

I'd have been out the window and down the street, as soon as I heard the piano playing inside the empty house at two in the morning.

But then I've got a very vivid imagination.

And, luckily, I've got a job where that's a good thing.

My dad trained himself out of having an imagination.

In his job, imagination was a hindrance.

Imagination got in the way and clouded your mind.

So you had to learn to control it.

You don't want to imagine things any other way than the simple facts.

And that's really good advice for everyday life.

Imagining what your boss thinks of you, worrying what the client's going to say, fretting over all the problems, all the things that might go wrong.

All of this can stop us doing great and exciting things.

But.

If we don't imagine things, how are we going to do our jobs?

How can we imagine a more creative kind of advertising?

A more exciting solution to any problem.

How can we imagine new ways to beat the competition?

Things that haven't been tried yet.

I think we have to have imagination.

But we have to make sure imagination doesn't have us.

We have to feed it, look after it, develop it.

Just like we would if we lived in Burma and needed an elephant to do our job.

It's vital to us, but we have to be in control of it.

We have to make sure the elephant does what we tell it to.

We can't let the elephant tell us what to do.

That's what happens if we let imagination get in control.

The good part of imagination is that you can take something and imagine what it would be like if it was more exciting.

The bad part of imagination is that you can take something and imagine what it would be like if it was more exciting.

In our business we need imagination.

As Rory Sutherland said, 'It's the job of advertising to make the new familiar, and the familiar new.'

And for that you need imagination.

Just remember, imagination makes a great servant and a lousy master.

Cock-up or conspiracy?

The *Bismarck* was the most powerful battleship in the world.

First time out, she utterly destroyed the pride of the Royal Navy, the *Hood*.

1,500 men died instantly.

Only three survived.

The best ship we had, gone in a second.

The Germans knew we had nothing to stop the *Bismarck*.

Until she was attacked by old Swordfish torpedo planes.

Ancient, rickety biplanes, so fragile they were nicknamed 'String-bags'.

They didn't even have a cockpit; the crew of three sat out in the open.

They flew at 90 mph, so slowly that the Bismarck's guns couldn't hit them.

The Bismarck had radar-controlled anti-aircraft guns, designed to shoot down modern planes, attacking at 250 mph.

Not bumbling old wood-and-fabric antiques.

One Swordfish launched its missile with the torpedo-aimer hanging upside down outside the fuselage while the gunner held his legs.

The torpedo hit and crippled the *Bismarck*'s rudder.

Which allowed the entire Royal Navy task force to catch up and sink her.

The most modern ship in the world brought down by something that belonged in a museum.

Cock-up over conspiracy.

During the same period of the war, Churchill tried everything he could to get America to supply Britain with arms.

He would meet with Roosevelt again and again.

And every time Roosevelt would agree.

But every time the weapons never came.

The pattern was always the same.

Churchill would state his request.

Roosevelt would nod enthusiastically and say, 'Yes, yes.'

Then later, the request would be denied.

Churchill couldn't work out what Roosevelt's game was.

Why was he misleading him, manipulating him, using him?

His deviousness, his cunning, constantly confused Churchill.

Recently, I saw an interview with Roosevelt's secretary.

He said, 'What Churchill never understood was that, when Roosevelt nodded his head and said, "Yes, yes," he wasn't necessarily agreeing. He was just indicating that he'd heard and understood what Churchill had said.'

Cock-up over conspiracy.

I think we're all guilty of that.

We spend all our time interpreting the world, instead of just listening.

I'm as guilty of that as anyone.

I failed at everything at school, so I grew up convinced I wasn't very smart.

Finally, at art school, I discovered advertising.

I knew it must be easy because I was good at it, and I was thick.

If I could do it, everybody must be able to.

So when I became a creative director, I developed a short fuse with people who wouldn't do what I wanted.

Knowing there was only one reason they wouldn't do it.

They must be lazy.

And there was no excuse for laziness.

Then one day my colleague Paul Bainsfair said to me, 'Dave, have you ever thought, maybe it isn't that people don't want to do what you want.

Maybe it's that they can't do what you want?'

I'd never thought of that.

Gradually a new thought dawned on me.

What if I wasn't thick?

In which case, maybe advertising wasn't as easy as I thought.

Maybe some people just couldn't do it.

Maybe they weren't being lazy after all.

And gradually it changed my view of the world.

Maybe the world isn't all conspiracy.

Maybe the world is just cock-up.

What we see says more about us than about what we see

About 50 years ago two teenagers broke into a factory at night.

One was 16 years old, Christopher Craig.

The other was 19, Derek Bentley.

Although Bentley was older, he was simple-minded.

He had what we'd now call 'learning difficulties'.

So Craig, although younger, was the leader.

However, neither of them was overly bright, and they were soon spotted.

Someone called the police.

When they arrived, Bentley (the older one) made a run for it.

But the police grabbed him and he gave up.

While the police were holding him, some distance away, Craig (the younger one) shot two policemen.

One of them died.

Both Craig and Bentley were tried for murder.

They were both found guilty.

Although Craig, the younger one, had fired the shots, he was under 18.

So he was too young to hang, and was sent to prison.

Although Bentley, the older one, was being held by police when the shots were fired, he was over 18.

So he was hanged for murder, even though he didn't fire the gun.

The evidence that got Bentley hanged was something he shouted at Craig.

A policeman approached Craig saying, 'Give me the gun, son.'

Bentley, being held by police, shouted, 'Let him have it, Chris.'

Bentley said he was encouraging Craig to give himself up.

And he was telling him to hand over the gun.

The prosecution said Bentley was using Hollywood slang, and he was actually telling Craig to shoot the copper.

That particular interpretation cost Bentley his life.

The truth is we can all see how those words could be interpreted either way.

We interpret words to mean what's already in our head.

We respond accordingly.

And usually what happens backs up our interpretation.

If we're stressed, we hear everything as an accusation.

We think what's going on in our head is actually what's happening in the outside world.

We don't even realize there's a difference.

Just this morning I was waiting at the traffic lights.

They went green and the bus in front of me didn't move.

I waited for another change of lights.

Still the bus didn't move.

I got out to see what was wrong.

Had it broken down?

Had it hit someone?

Had the bus driver collapsed?

I walked up to the driver's window and said, 'What's the problem, mate?'

He started waving his arms angrily at me and said, 'Where the fuck am I gonna go, eh? You tell me, where the fuck am I gonna go?'

I looked around and there was a tar-laying machine in front.

I said, 'Can't you get round it, then?'

He said furiously, 'How the fuck do you think I can get round that? Can you drive a bus, eh?'

All the bus driver could hear were people sounding their horns.

He was frustrated and stressed.

So he didn't hear me asking, 'What's the problem, mate?'

It was a genuine question.

He heard me accusing him, 'Get a move on, dope, anyone can drive a bus through a gap that big.'

Because that reinforced his reality.

And we all do that every day.

In every interaction.

Create a reality.

Misinterpret it.

Then reinforce it.

As the author Anaïs Nin said, 'We see things not as they are,
but as we are.

Push-thinking vs pull-thinking

The Michelin Guide is the most influential indicator of a restaurant's quality.

If a restaurant has a single Michelin star it can charge pretty much what it wants.

If it has two Michelin stars the queue will be round the block.

If it has three Michelin stars you'll have to book a year ahead.

The great chefs train their whole lives to achieve, and then hang on to, Michelin stars.

But the Michelin Guide didn't start out as a guide to cuisine.

It started out as a way of selling tyres.

In 1900 the Michelin brothers owned a tyre company in France.

They wanted to sell more tyres.

And, in order to do that, they needed to get drivers to wear down the ones they had.

So in 1900 they issued the first Michelin Guide.

It showed all the great things to see and do around France.

It encouraged people to get out in their cars and drive to all these places.

It featured a list of sights to see, places to buy petrol, places to stay.

The locations of garages, mechanics.

And, being French, good places to eat.

So the Michelin Guide wasn't originally just about restaurants.

It was a list of reasons to travel.

That's why the original meaning of the star rating for restaurants was as follows.

1 star: worth stopping for.

2 stars: worth a detour.

3 stars: worth a special journey.

The guide was a phenomenal success.

So much so that it had to be printed and updated regularly due to demand.

But its popularity created its own problems.

Originally, when they started the guide, it was given away for free.

They updated it every year at their own cost.

As a marketing tool, it seemed a good investment.

But after about 20 years it had stopped being a novelty.

It was taken for granted.

One of the brothers spotted a pile of Michelin Guides in a garage forecourt.

Being used to prop up a table.

He was outraged.

It wasn't being treated with respect.

Because people don't value things that come too easily.

So the brothers stopped giving it away for free.

They began charging for it.

It meant there were fewer in circulation.

And because they had to be bought, people looked after them.

They wouldn't loan them, or throw them away.

All of this had the effect of making it more respected.

More of an authority.

And the Michelin Guide assumed a life of its own.

Away from anything to do with tyres, or motoring, or garages.

Now consumers looked to it for guidance on a restaurant's quality.

This meant chefs fought to get into it, and they fought for higher ratings.

The successful ones, loving awards, displayed their stars prominently.

Consumers, seeing that top chefs took it seriously, treated it as an authority.

The Michelin Guide is a great example of Choice Architecture.

Pull-thinking rather than push-thinking.

Instead of constantly nagging people to use your product, it shows them something they'd love to do.

Something that needn't even involve mentioning your product.

Something fun.

And incidentally, without even mentioning it, you've created a need for more sales of your product.

And, if you get it right, you might create something that's so good it takes on a life of its own.

In which case you've not only got a great piece of marketing. You've got a whole new business.

The only medium that doesn't change is people

The future is more uncertain than it's ever been.

Technology is going to change everything beyond recognition.

The times we're living through are unlike anything that can even be imagined.

The new will change and/or replace all current knowledge.

According to all the new-media gurus, everything that was previously known is dinosaur thinking.

And not just in technology.

Here are some quotes from famous people that prove we're living in a world unlike anything that's ever existed.

Everything is moving at such an accelerated pace, current knowledge is out of date.

See if you can guess which famous person made the following statements about our world.

See what you think about their views.

Quote 1

'I see no hope for the future of our people if they are dependent on the youth of today.

All modern youths are reckless beyond words.

When I was young, we were taught to be respectful of elders, but the youth of today is the opposite: totally disrespectful.'

Quote 2

'The young now love only luxury.

They have bad manners, contempt for authority, and show disrespect for their elders.

They lounge around when anyone enters the room.

They argue with their parents, interrupt everyone, scoff their food and terrorize their teachers.'

Quote 3

'The world is passing through troubled times.

The young people of today think of nothing but themselves ...

They talk as if they knew everything, and what passes for wisdom with us is foolishness to them.'

Quote 4

'In a pub, there sat 40 to 50 young people of both sexes, nearly all under 17 years old ...

Among them were openly confessed professional prostitutes. No wonder that early sexual intercourse and youthful prostitution, beginning at 14 to 15 years old, is extraordinarily frequent. Crimes of a savage and desperate sort are a common occurrence.'

The one thing these famous people are agreed on is the fashion for ridiculing or ignoring all former knowledge. Anyone who isn't part of the new way of doing things is a dinosaur and can safely be ignored.

It's an unsettling state of affairs.

But understandable given the world has never seen anything like it before.

So who are these experts on the way our world is going?

Quote 1: Hesiod (a contemporary of Homer) in c.700 BC.

Quote 2: Socrates in c.380 BC.

Quote 3: Peter the Hermit in 1274.

Quote 4: Friedrich Engels in 1844.

Yup, the world's changing so much it's unrecognizable.

No one's ever seen anything like it before.

PART TEN

THE JOURNEY IS THE DESTINATION

The journey vs the destination

Mick Dean was a very successful advertising photographer.
He won lots of awards, owned a very nice studio, made lots of money, bought pretty much whatever he wanted and generally had a good life.
Mick is also an intelligent, thoughtful bloke.
He likes to read a lot.
Especially about history.
Mick read about the ancient pilgrimage trail to Santiago de Compostela.
A route pilgrims have walked for over 1,000 years.
Starting in a small village in France, and going on foot across the Pyrenees into Spain.
Over 600 miles, all the way to an ancient cathedral in a small town.
Mick was intrigued with the idea of walking the route.
He loved the history of it.
Not just third-hand history from the pages of a book.
Mick liked the idea of connecting directly with history, being a part of it.
Putting your feet exactly where those ancient people put their feet.
Feeling the wind on your face exactly as they did.
Smelling the fields exactly as they did.

Almost like time travel.

A chance to actually be there.

But, like a lot of things in life we're fascinated with, we know we'll never actually do it.

Real life takes over.

We're too busy, we've got too many jobs on, too much work, too many deadlines.

And he put it on the back burner.

But then strange coincidences began happening to Mick.

In a restaurant, he mentioned it to a friend of his.

The friend said he'd read the book too, and he'd love to do it.

But Mick's friend was very sick and knew he'd never be able to walk that distance.

As they talked someone at the next table leaned across.

They said, 'I hope you don't mind me interrupting, but I couldn't help overhearing.

It's possible to travel that route on horseback, you know.'

And they began giving Mick details.

What are the chances of that?

And gaps began opening up, at work and in Mick's private life.

Gradually, a month appeared on his calendar when nothing was happening.

It felt to Mick like he was being pointed towards this.

Mick began to get the feeling that he was supposed to do this walk.

And eventually he gave in.

And Mick, leading his friend on a horse, began to walk back into history.

The walk still takes about three weeks, just as it did 1,000 years ago.

Mick said it was a life-changing experience for him.

He'd never done anything like that before.

Never intentionally slowed everything down.

Never allowed every tiny detail of something to gradually unfold at its own pace.

Normally, Mick would just look at the purpose of the journey.

Then get to the end point as quickly and efficiently as possible.

The end point of the pilgrimage was the cathedral at Santiago de Compostela.

So Mick would normally get a cab to Heathrow, a flight to the nearest Spanish airport, then a cab to the cathedral.

See the cathedral, and get a flight back.

You could do it all in a day.

How could it make any kind of sense to spend three weeks doing something that could be condensed into eight hours?

And it dawned on Mick that his whole life had become about the result, about getting to the end.

The bit until he got to the end was just something to minimize as much as possible, in order to get the result faster.

All that counted was the end of the process, not the process itself.

And Mick thought, what is the purpose of life, the end of the process?

Well, for all of us there is only one possible end to the process.

And we won't be around for that.

So effectively the end doesn't exist.

Like the walk to Santiago de Compostela.

Once you get to the cathedral, the walk is over.

The walk itself, the purpose of the journey, is finished.

Mick saw that the journey was the destination.

He'd been living his whole life for something that didn't even exist.

And, in stretching a two-hour plane journey into a three-week walking journey, Mick realized what he wanted his life to be about.

He wanted it to be about the journey, the part that actually existed.

Not about the end, the part that didn't exist.

And Mick came back to London and gave up being a photographer.

He went to art school to become a painter.

And now Mick spends every day doing what he loves.

He enjoys every second of the journey.

Of course he doesn't make anything like so much money.

He doesn't win awards, or have big cars, or a big house, or expensive clothes.

What happened to Mick on that walk was he got to see the end of the journey.

And he got to think, 'When it's all over, what will I wish I'd done?'

Then he thought, 'If I'll wish I'd done it when it's too late, why don't I just do it now?'

Logic is our superstition

When we first got married, my wife and I were doing the washing up.

She was doing it very fast.

But I didn't think we were doing it as well as we could.

So I stopped, and I said, 'Cath, there's not enough room on the draining board for all the wet crockery. But if we wash the small things first, we can stack the big bowls on top of them, and we'll have more room.'

But Cathy wasn't listening.

By the time I'd finished explaining my thinking, Cathy had finished the washing up and was doing something else.

See, Cathy is geared towards action rather than talk.

Results rather than reasons.

Cathy's mum once said to me, 'In the West you love to talk and talk, and think things over. But we Chinese prefer to just get it done.'

When I first went to the Far East I was amazed at the amount of superstition.

Every building had to have feng shui performed on it.

Every building had a little Taoist shrine in front of it.

I used to think, these people are very superstitious.

Not like us in the West, we're logical.

Then one day it occurred to me.

They're not actually any more superstitious than us.

We've just got different superstitions, that's all.

Logic is our superstition.

We believe in logic above all else.

If logic says it will work, that's enough.

Faith will override the evidence of results.

That's just like any religion or superstition.

In primitive tribes the medicine man is the person who cures people.

It's that simple.

If he can cure you, he's the medicine man.

Whether he's been trained or not.

We regard this as primitive because, in the West, it's the other way round.

In the West, the medicine man is the person who's had the training.

The person who's got the piece of paper on the wall, saying he's the medicine man.

Whether he can actually cure you or not is irrelevant.

He's the man who has been qualified as the medicine man.

Whether it works or not.

The logic of why it should work is important.

The results are secondary.

It's the same with scientists, lawyers, accountants, engineers.

The person who must be good at the job is the person who's had the training.

The person who's got the diploma, the degree, the piece of paper.

It's the same with advertising.

We depend on what should work, not what does work.

If an ad campaign is researched enough, it should work.

That's that.

Of course we can point to ad campaigns that worked without being researched.

But we see that as a bit amateur.

Lucky, a one off.

It doesn't fit with our superstition.

Akio Morita, the founder of Sony, said, 'The greatest assistance I had in building my company was the total failure of nerve on the part of Western businessmen to move without research.'

Richard Branson has a similar attitude.

He says at Virgin they explore lots of different things.

If something excites them they go ahead and try it.

Lots of these are failures.

But about one in five is a massive success.

And, before they did it, they couldn't identify which one that was going to be.

So they try them all.

Because if they tried to avoid having the failures, they wouldn't have the successes.

Steve Jobs, founder of Apple, had a similar view.

He didn't believe in research.

He said, 'It's not the public's job to know what they're going to want. It's my job to know what they're going to want.'

The secret to being a creative director

The best advice I ever heard about being a creative director was from Kenny Dalglish.

He was Liverpool's all-time greatest player.

He won the FA Cup and the European Super Cup.

He won the Charity Shield five times.

He won the League (the equivalent of the Premiership) six times.

He won the European Cup three times.

Eventually, he became interested in the next step in his career.

Being a manager.

He thought he'd have to stop playing to learn this new trade.

But Liverpool wanted to hang on to him for as long as they could.

So they suggested a compromise.

He could be a 'player-manager'.

He could play for Liverpool and, at the same time, be their manager.

So that's what Dalglish did.

He played regularly for Liverpool while learning how to put together, and run, a team.

One day he was being interviewed by the press.

A journalist asked him, 'How are you finding the transition to management, Kenny?'

In a heavy Scottish accent Dalglish said, 'Well, I'll know I've got the team right when I can't get on it.'

And there it is.

The single best piece of advice about being a creative director.

You get the creative director's job because usually, like Kenny Dalglish, you're really good at what you do.

You're a terrific art director or copywriter.

You do great ads.

But being a creative director, like being a football manager, is a different job.

Now the job isn't to go on the pitch and score yourself.

Now the job is to put together a team that can score without you.

The temptation is to carry on doing great ads yourself.

But that isn't a creative director's job.

That's a copywriter or art director.

Of course you're capable of doing ads yourself, that isn't the question.

The question is, can you get other people to do it?

If you can't, you're not really a creative director.

You're still a copywriter or art director.

Of course the problem is the same as it was for Kenny Dalglish.

You're actually better than some of the people in the team.

You know you could do better ads yourself than some of the work they're showing you.

So what do you do?

You can't let bad ads run, that doesn't help anyone.

Well, the difference between us and Kenny Dalglish is that we haven't got 60,000 people watching our every move.

So it depends how badly you want to be a creative director.

If you want it badly enough, sometimes you might have to do the work yourself and pretend the team did it.

Because you don't want to be known for just doing good ads any more.

Now you want to be known for running a department that turns out good ads.

Of course this is difficult.

It's always difficult to give away credit for something you've done yourself.

To put someone else's name down as writer or art director.

But just make sure your name goes down as creative director.

That way you'll be known for what you want to be known for.

Incidentally, how did this approach work for Kenny Dalglish?

How did he do as manager of Liverpool?

He won the FA Cup twice.

He won the Charity Shield four times.

He won the League three times running.

As Kenny Dalglish said, you'll know you've got the team right when you can't get on it.

HAVE-DO-BE vs BE-DO-HAVE

I always look at everything as rungs on a ladder.

You're never going to jump straight to the top of the ladder.

If you try you keep failing, and eventually give up.

So personally, I believe in going up the ladder one rung at a time.

When I got my job as a junior copywriter at BMP, I knew I eventually wanted to be a creative director.

One rung down from that was deputy creative director.

One rung down from that was group head.

One rung down from that was copywriter, which was me.

So my next step up must be group head.

But my Executive Creative Director, John Webster, didn't see it that way.

He said that was the structure of old-fashioned uncreative agencies.

And he didn't want that at BMP.

He wanted a flat structure of copywriter and art director teams.

And one creative director: him.

Well, that definitely made sense creatively.

Problem was it didn't fit my agenda.

So how to go about changing it?

All I wanted, to start, was a little junior team working under me.

Then at least I'd have the beginnings of a group.

But arguing about it was not going to get him to change his mind.

So I thought, let's help John to have the idea himself.

And so I started taking on a lot of work.

I mean a lot of work.

And I started getting in student placement teams to help me do it.

And pretty soon I had a little group.

And we were getting lots of work out.

And eventually John spotted it.

And he said to me, 'You can't carry on doing all this work on your own. Why don't you hire a junior team to help you?'

And, effectively, I was a group head.

See, how most people think the world works is HAVE-DO-BE.

They would say they can't BE a group head until they HAVE the title.

If they HAVE the title, they'll DO the work involved, and they'll eventually BE performing as a group head.

They operate the HAVE-DO-BE principle.

So they try to get someone to give them the title.

And sometimes they wait their whole life and never get it.

I didn't have the time or the inclination to do it that way.

So I took the other route.

BE-DO-HAVE.

I decided I would BE a group head, and I would DO all the work of a group head, and eventually I would HAVE the job title.

For me, doing the job comes first, the title comes second.

So that's the sort of people I've always promoted.

People who are already doing the job rather than waiting for someone to give them the title.

People who just get on with it, instead of waiting for permission.

For me it's the advertising equivalent of a bunch of men digging up the road.

There will always be one man down the hole digging, and two or three men standing around the top watching.

The person you promote is the one down the hole digging.

Not the ones up the top watching.

I used to notice that a lot of secretaries were grumpy, and didn't enjoy their jobs.

I used to ask them why they were doing the job if they hated it.

They usually said they were only doing it because they wanted to get into the TV department and become a producer.

This is the HAVE-DO-BE principle at work.

She's not going to do a good job until someone gives her the title she wants.

Well, let's see how that works.

Is it possible that the head of TV is thinking, 'What we really need is a grumpy secretary who hates her job and does it badly. So we can train her up to be a TV producer.'

I doubt it.

At my old agency GGT we had a creative secretary called Diane Croll.

She was a brilliant secretary.

So we asked her to liaise with the freelance producers and production companies we were using.

And she did that job brilliantly as well.

So we asked her to be our TV producer.

And she did that brilliantly, too.

Whatever job you gave her, however small, she did it brilliantly.

And she became head of TV and in charge of six other producers.

And, eventually, a member of the board.

She wasn't HAVE-DO-BE.

She was definitely BE-DO-HAVE.

Ask yourself what sort of person you'd prefer to be.

And what sort of person you'd prefer to have working for you.

Reasonable people

I was listening to Dame Ellen MacArthur on *Desert Island Discs*.

She became the youngest person ever to sail single-handedly, non-stop, around the world.

The interviewer asked who her inspirations were.

She said, 'My grandmother was very influential.'

The interviewer asked why.

Ellen MacArthur said, 'She always wanted to go to university, and in fact she won a scholarship to pay for her to go.

But her father, my great-grandfather, wouldn't allow her to go.

They were a poor family, and he said she needed to get a job to bring money into the household.

So she did, but later she made sure her three daughters went to university.

And she was so fascinated with learning that every day, when I was young, she used to come to my school and sit in the canteen with me and my friends.

Then, when she was old and retired, and at the end of her life, she went back to university to get a degree.

And she finally graduated three months before she died.'

So there's a clue to where Ellen MacArthur got the determination to sail a ship, that should have been crewed by a dozen men, for 71 days.

Alone.

Thousands of miles from anywhere.

The nearest land 7 miles straight down.

The waves twice as high as the average house.

Sleeping a few minutes at a time, always on deck.

The interviewer asked her about her first boat.

How did she get it?

She said it was a tiny little dinghy and she saved up for it.

'We didn't get any pocket money when we were little.

So, anything we wanted, we either had to make it or save up for it.

I used to save the change from my school-dinner money every day.'

The interviewer asked her to elaborate.

She said, 'Every day I'd eat beans, mashed potato and gravy.

Beans cost four pence, mashed potato cost four pence, gravy was free.

So I'd have the beans and mash swimming in gravy, almost like soup.

Everyone thought I was crazy. But I'd go home and stack the change up next to my savings tin.

When the change reached £1, I'd put it in my savings tin.

Then I'd fill in one of the little squares on a sheet of graph paper I had on the wall.

When I had 100 little squares filled in I'd take the money to the building society.'

The interviewer asked her how much her first boat cost.

She said, '£535.'

And you get another clue to the level of determination she considered normal.

The interviewer then asked what life had been like at home.

She said she'd been very happy at home, if slightly unconventional.

The interviewer asked for an example.

She said, 'Well, I only had a very small bedroom.

There really wasn't room in it for the bed plus everything else I was making and storing.

So when my parents went out one day, I took the bed apart and put it in the barn.

I figured, if I asked them, they were likely to object.

But if I did it while they were out it would be a fait accompli.

And from then on, I just slept on the floor in a sleeping bag, and had lots more room for everything I wanted to do in my bedroom.'

You get another clue to the sort of determination that could make her climb to the top of a mast six storeys high.

On her own in the middle of the ocean.

With the ship speeding along at 40 mph in the pitch dark.

And fix a broken block-and-tackle in sub-zero temperature.

You see, none of what she did was reasonable behaviour.

Not saving £500 from her lunch money.

Not throwing her bed out of her bedroom.

Not sailing single-handedly, non-stop, around the world.

What I loved about listening to her was that she didn't let other people's ideas of what was reasonable dictate her behaviour.

She looked at the problem.

Worked out what she thought was the best way of proceeding.

Then, if it made sense to her, she went ahead and did it.

Whatever anyone else said.

She didn't let other people's version of what was reasonable stop her.

She came to her own conclusion.

How many of us do that?

How many of us question what we're told and come to our own conclusions?

Don't we usually just do what we're told?

Reasonable people don't do what she did.

Not the big things, not even the little things.

Because reasonable people just want to fit in.

So they don't question what other people tell them.

But then reasonable people don't do much.

Speaking the unspeakable

Years ago Cindy Gallop was an account manager at GGT.

More recently, she used to be CEO of BBH in New York.

She was voted Ad Woman of the Year by the New York
equivalent of *Campaign*.

Recently I saw Cindy do a talk at TED.

She was launching a project she feels strongly about.

A website called Make Love Not Porn.

Cindy spoke in front of several hundred top decision-makers.

In cut-glass English pronunciation she explained that she was
on older woman who liked to date young men.

She explained that 'date' was a euphemism for 'have sex
with'.

So Cindy liked to have sex with young men.

A lot of young men.

She didn't see why talking about that should be a problem.

But what was a problem was that young men had their
complete view of sex dictated by Internet porn.

An entire generation was growing up to believe that what
they saw on porn sites was the way it should be.

They saw men with enormous penises, and women loving it.

So obviously that was the way it should be.

They saw women enjoying gagging on these enormous
penises.

Then enjoying being spanked and sodomized.

Being that this was the total extent of most young men's sex education, this was what they believed all women enjoyed.

And young women were also being educated by the same Internet porn as their boyfriends.

So they believed there must be something wrong with them if they didn't enjoy it.

Cindy thought this was wrong.

Not that Internet porn was wrong.

She quite enjoyed that.

But she didn't think it should dictate what everyone should, or shouldn't, want.

It should be OK for different people to want different things.

So she set up a website to educate young people.

To open up the debate.

But TED was shocked by Cindy's talk.

They wouldn't make it available on their main website.

The subject matter was too contentious.

So Cindy persuaded them to make it available on YouTube.

Some of the comments it attracted were rational.

But some were barely literate insults.

The sort of thing you'd normally see written on the door of a public lavatory.

But Cindy didn't get angry like I would have.

And she didn't delete the comments like I would have.

Her attitude is, 'We see the world not as it is, but as we are.'

So she figured people who would make these sort of comments are actually having real problems.

Maybe she could help sort them out.

She's had around 800 comments.

So far she's replied to over 200 of them.

She replied personally to each insulting comment.

Asking them to contact her at her email address to continue the discussion.

As you can imagine, this is not what people who comment anonymously want.

So most of the debates ended there.

However, to illustrate her point she told me about one particular comment.

A guy had written something like, 'Looking at a wrinkled old hag like you, who would want to come on your face anyway?'

Cindy, believing the guy only wrote that because of problems in his personal life, asked him to get in touch by email.

It turned out he was a 28-year-old virgin, living in Eastern Europe.

During their correspondence he told Cindy that he couldn't get a girlfriend.

Cindy suggested he try Internet dating.

She gave him tips on how to proceed.

Recently he wrote back to thank her.

Saying he now had a girlfriend, and he was in love.

Cindy believes that a lot of male anger and problems come from testosterone and pent-up sexual rage.

She says, 'There aren't many problems in the world that couldn't be cured by blow jobs.'

I don't agree.

I think there are lots of problems that couldn't be cured by blow jobs.

But I think I learned from Cindy that maybe there are a lot of problems that could be cured that way.

Something else I learned was that it's not always best to meet anger with anger.

Rage fuels rage.

It's a purely emotional reaction.

Eventually the stronger side wins.

But even if you win, you lose.

You lose control of yourself and the situation.

Cindy meets anger with understanding.

The rational mind.

That either dissolves the anger, because the rage has nowhere to go.

Or it solves the anger by helping address the problem.

I can't always do that myself.

In fact I can't do it very often.

But I wish I could.

What if it really was a matter of life and death?

The opening 20 minutes of *Saving Private Ryan* is the best war sequence ever.

That's because Spielberg based it on ten famous photographs of D-Day.

But why are there only ten photographs of an event of such historical significance?

The photographer was Robert Capa.

He went in on one of the first landing craft.

It hit the sandy bottom about 100 yards from the shore.

The ramp went down.

The men jumped out as the bullets came in.

Capa crouched on the ramp taking photos.

The boat captain kicked him in the arse, off the boat and into the surf.

So the boat could get the hell out of there.

Capa struggled through the surf to get to the shore.

All the soldier's equipment, and the knee-deep surf, made it hard to move, like in a dream.

When you want to run but your feet are like lead.

Which made them an easier target for the German machine-gunners in the pillboxes.

Capa and the other soldiers tried to shelter from the bullets behind the landing obstacles.

Crude shapes made from steel girders welded together like a giant X.

As he crouched there, he took more photographs.

Shots of other soldiers crouching.

Shots of soldiers crawling through the surf.

Some dead, some wounded, some firing, some running.

He photographed everything he possibly could.

When he'd used up all his film, he ran back out into the surf.

Another landing craft came in, the ramp came down, the men jumped out.

Capa ran up the ramp and yelled that he was a war photographer, and he wanted to get back to get his pictures developed.

So, having gone in with the first wave at Omaha Beach, he got out alive.

With three rolls of film, 108 pictures, of the greatest invasion the world has ever seen.

He got back to London and took the film to the offices of *LIFE* magazine.

Where a 15-year-old lab assistant turned the heating up too high in the drier.

And it melted all the emulsion and virtually all the film was destroyed.

They only managed to save ten photographs out of the 108 that Capa took.

Imagine that.

90% of your work gone.

You've just risked your life in the biggest battle of the war.

Hundreds of ships, thousands of planes, tens of thousands of men.

All going head-to-head in a vast, cataclysmic confrontation.

And you're right in the middle of it with your camera.

A once-in-a-lifetime opportunity.

You risk your life to capture every frame.

All around you thousands of soldiers die, but you get back alive.

And it was all for nothing.

What do you do?

What can you do?

You can't reshoot it.

You can't do D-Day again.

That's it.

Nearly all your work, everything you risked your life for, gone.

I think it's worth remembering that.

Next time we lose an ad because planning turns it down.

Or the account man can't sell it.

Or the client won't buy it.

Or Clearcast turn the script down.

It's good to get it all in perspective.

Denial

When I was at art school in Brooklyn, I was looking for an apartment to share.
One guy I went to see was a bodybuilder with rippling muscles.
He was about 30 and, at the time, that seemed really old to me.
He said he was gay and did I have a problem with that?
I said I wasn't and I didn't.
He told me he used to go 'straight-bashing' at the weekends.
I asked what that was.
He said he'd get a small, gay friend of his to go around various bars and act really camp.
Meanwhile he would wait outside.
Eventually some drunks would start picking on the little guy.
Calling him faggot and shoving him around.
When they took him outside to beat him up, this guy would be waiting.
And he'd kick the daylights out of them.
Fair enough.
He told me he was actually bisexual.
He said, in his time, he'd had sex with around 500 women and 1,500 men.
Fair enough.

I didn't end up sharing a flat with him.

But one thing he told me did come in very useful.

He said the canteen at my college was the biggest 'cruising' venue in New York City.

It came in useful because one of my courses was psychology.

And to pass, we had to write a thesis.

This meant coming up with a question.

Interviewing lots of people and drawing conclusions from the results.

Basically, crude research.

For a creative person this could be a dull process.

Unless I could find an interesting and provocative question.

Now I knew the college canteen was full of gay men that was easier.

I made my title something like, 'Gay: nature or nurture?'

I had lots of potential subjects to interview.

I'd ask them all about their history, when did they know they were gay, patterns of behaviour, etc.

This is many years ago now, but I remember one thing that surprised me.

The majority of these guys had lived in denial about it for a long time.

They'd had sex with many more females than a straight guy would have.

Until they stopped resisting and admitted they were gay.

Ever since then, I've thought the subject of denial is fascinating.

How we try to impose our will about our self-image on the physical universe.

Without looking at the evidence.

I was in denial about advertising when I was young.

I thought it was just big business manipulating the gullible masses.

I thought I should be involved in something better.

Like joining the Peace Corps and serving in the Third World.

But the evidence said I was good at advertising.

I was in denial.

I spent years resisting it.

Eventually I came out of the closet.

I admitted to myself that I loved advertising.

When we come out of the closet, about whatever it is, we release all the energy we previously wasted in pretence and denial.

We can start enjoying what we always wanted to do.

And that's a better way to spend our time on the planet.

So the question was, could I be in advertising and help the Third World?

Well, if you're creative there's always a way.

Media doesn't have to be media

Oxfam asked the top people in UK advertising to a briefing
on Third World debt.

They explained that during the lending boom banks had
loaned billions to Third World countries at extortionate
interest rates.

They explained that merely paying the interest on the debt
was bankrupting the poorest countries.

Consequently the IMF enforced austerity measures on these
countries.

These measures are directly responsible for 500,000 infant
deaths a year.

Oxfam couldn't get involved as the issue was political not
charitable.

The challenge to us was to raise the debate around getting
the debt cancelled.

We made and ran dozens of commercials, posters and press
ads for free.

But we had to get the message inside the high-street banks.

How to do that when there is no media inside the banks?

No TV, no radio, no press ads, no posters.

We found one thing that the banks are full of, that could be
changed into media.

Paper money.

We got small printing kits from Ryman and printed:
'STOP BANKS KILLING CHILDREN. CANCEL THE THIRD WORLD
DEBT' on every bank note we could get hold of.

Printing any message on that money was considered
defacing it.

Defacing currency is illegal and it has to be taken out of
circulation.

To take a banknote out of circulation requires filling in a
form in quadruplicate.

These forms each go to four different departments, which
each fill out more forms in quadruplicate.

So each defaced bank note ensures the message replicates
itself at least 20 times throughout the bank.

When we started working on it, no one had heard of the
Third World debt crisis.

Now, lots of people have, and it is a matter of public debate.

Many became involved in stamping their money, and each
person makes a difference.

Just on my own, I've stamped that message on many bank
notes every month.

So I've got that message reproduced inside the banks
thousands of times.

It's a great example of the way an individual can be
empowered.

Instead of thinking they can't do anything.

EPILOGUE:
LEARNING ISN'T THE SAME
AS BEING TAUGHT

My wife's dad was born in China around 1916.

I say 'around' because no one's exactly sure.

In 1922, when he was a small boy, a massive flood obliterated the entire region.

It destroyed all the villages, and drowned everyone who lived there.

It was known as the Great Typhoon of Swatow.

They estimate that up to 100,000 people died.

Again, they don't know exact numbers.

All my father-in-law remembered was that for three days and nights he clung to a tree.

A little boy on his own.

All he could see was water, as far as the horizon in every direction.

Eventually he was rescued and taken to an orphanage.

He thinks he was somewhere around five or six years old.

His entire family had been wiped out along with everyone else.

But after a year an uncle came looking for him.

This uncle had missed the floods, because he was away working on the rice boats between Thailand and Singapore.

So at about eight years old, my father-in-law went with his uncle to work on the rice boats.

After a few years he decided he liked Singapore so much he stayed there.

Working at anything that came his way.

Buying and selling things, fixing things, transporting things.

Whatever wanted doing, he would do it.

Everything was an opportunity.

Despite the fact that he couldn't read or write, mechanical things made sense to him.

He trained himself in electrics, plumbing, engines, building, drainage.

He just looked for every opportunity and did it, whatever it was.

He never read a book, or passed a test, or studied for a qualification.

How could he?

He'd never been to school so he couldn't read or write.

Eventually he opened his own company, a plumbing contractor.

He didn't do the work to industry standards.

He'd never learned anyone else's standards.

He did it to his own standards, how he thought it should be done.

It turned out his standards were higher than anyone else's.

And his company became one of the biggest in Singapore.

He decided his suppliers' quality wasn't good enough.

So he started making whatever he needed, himself.

He opened a stainless-steel factory and a cast-iron foundry.

His business had grown so much, he needed bigger offices.

But he couldn't find a builder he thought was good enough.

So he did it himself.

He built a massive office block for his company headquarters.

Without being able to read or write he'd somehow assembled a huge plumbing and building conglomerate.

All because he looked at what everyone else was doing and decided it wasn't good enough.

Even though he'd never been taught how to do it.

In fact, *because* he'd never been taught how to do it.

I believe that was his strength, that he had no training.

He couldn't read and write, he'd never been to school.

He'd never had anyone else teach him the right way to do it.

He had to work it out for himself.

Sort out what made sense to him and what didn't.

He wasn't just another product of the educational conveyor belt, where someone else tells you exactly what can and can't be done.

What the limitations are.

What's acceptable and what isn't.

Creativity must be about questioning the way things are, and doing them differently.

You can't do that if you've had all the questioning knocked out of you.

If all you've learned is to regurgitate the expected answers.

The academic world doesn't have the same opportunities as the real world.

In the real world there isn't a teacher to mark your paper.

There isn't a set agenda to be marked against.

There aren't recognised criteria to memorize.

In the real world there's getting a result against the competition.

That's the real world.

Finding a creative way to out-think other people.

Entrepreneurialism crossed with creativity.

Otherwise known as predatory thinking.

I would like to thank my editor, Jon Butler, and all his colleagues at Macmillan, and I'd also like to thank my literary agent, Jonathan Conway. I felt like the first runner in a relay race, passing the baton on to them.